The Horse in War

In dreary, doubtful waiting hours
Before the brazen frenzy starts,
The horses show him nobler powers:
O patient eyes, courageous hearts!

Julian Grenfell, *Into Battle*

The Horse in War

J M Brereton

Arco Publishing Company, Inc.
New York

I am indebted to many individuals and institutions for valuable help in preparing this book, and, while it is impossible to list them all, I must single out the following for their generosity: Mr V. Bernacki, Mrs R. Blenman-Bull, Mr E. G. Butler, Mr H. V. Musgrave Clark, Mr G. D. Deakin, Captain R. S. J. Dembinski, Lieutenant-Colonel K. Krzeczunowicz, Brigadier J. P. Randle OBE, MC, Major Franz Thiele.

My chapters on the American scene would have been the poorer without the kindness of friends in the United States, among them: Mr A. E. Lueddeke, Dr Richard Pearse, Miss June F. Cunningham (Virginia Military Institute), Mr Gene M. Gressley (University of Wyoming), Miss Katherine Schaefer (University of Montana).

I owe much to the librarians of The London Library and Royal United Services Institute for references, while special thanks are due to Mr K. M. White of The Staff College Library, Camberley.

Finally, for constant encouragement and informed comment on equestrian matters, I thank my wife who shares my love of horses.

Published by Arco Publishing Company, Inc.
219 Park Avenue South, New York, N.Y. 10003

Copyright © 1976 by J. M. Brereton

Library of Congress Cataloging in Publication Data
Brereton, John Maurice.
    The horse in war.
    Bibliography: p.
    Includes index.
    1. Cavalry—History. 2. Horses—History.
I. Title.
UE15.B73   1976   357'.1   76-866
ISBN 0-668-03959-0
Printed in Great Britain

Contents

Preface

The horse is by nature one of the most timid and nervous species of our animal world. Despite the conceptions of non-horsemen—and some old-time cavalry recruits—he is not normally aggressive; if menaced, his instinctive reaction is instant flight. Though armed with powerful jaws and even more powerful hindquarters, he seldom regards these as potential weapons preferring discretion to valour. What sort of a creature is this, then, to carry a warrior among the tumult and the shouting, the roar of cannon, the scream of shell?

Yet throughout recorded history the horse has been man's most loyal and steadfast ally in battle. He has patiently suffered untold terror, and dreadful multilation; he has galloped unflinchingly into valleys of death; he has borne the captains and the kings and their armed cohorts to the ends of the earth, enabling them to carve out their empires. No other animal has exerted such profound influence on the affairs of mankind; without the horse, the pattern of world history would surely have been otherwise.

There are those still living who have thrilled to the spectacle of a cavalry regiment or horse artillery battery thundering past a saluting base. Perhaps they will sigh for the 'plumed pomp' that is vanished, perhaps recall with nostalgia the unique comradeship that was bred of the horse, in war and peace; but very likely they will forget the other side of the picture. The glorious battles of the past spelt misery and horror, not only for man but for beast. We may still honour the Light Brigade; but when we marvel at the 'gallant six hundred', do we not tend to overlook the charger and the troop horse that carried them so gallantly?

The field of military history abounds in literature on the mounted arm, but it is sad that all too often the services of its intrinsic component, the horse, receive scant acknowledgement. In this book I have tried to pay a little of the tribute due to the equine partner in that remarkable man-mount relationship which was the essence of the horse-soldier through the ages.

Man into Horseman

If the modern Thoroughbred could be confronted with what humans claim to be his original ancestor he would doubtless recoil in horrified indignation. All authorities are agreed that the story of the horse begins about 55 million years ago with a curious little creature known appropriately as Eohippus—'dawn horse'. To our eyes Eohippus would not be recognisable as a member of the horse family. During his lifetime there was no primitive human species to scratch his outline on cave walls or desert rocks, but extraordinarily well-preserved fossilised skeletons have given us a very good idea of what he looked like in that Eocene—'new dawn'—epoch. At first he was no bigger than a large fox, some 10in high at the shoulders, but later he developed to about twice that size. Thus, a horseman might say he stood anything from about 2.2 to 5 hands. His rather ungainly body was covered with short hair; the hindquarters were higher than the forehand, and this feature, together with a steeply arched back, gave him a distinctly rabbit-

How it all began: an artist's conception of Eophippus, based on fossilised remains

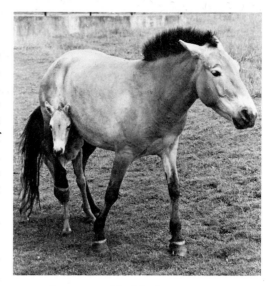

like appearance. The head, too, set on a short, thick neck, had a rabbit's snout, and was tipped with small rounded ears.

Eohippus was at first indigenous to what is now the southern part of the United States. Later, before the coming of the Ice Age, he spread throughout North America, and by way of the land-bridge that then existed in place of the present Bering Sea, he penetrated into Europe. This quaint little 'cony beast' eventually evolved into *Equus caballus*, or the horse, and with the advent of the Pleistocene epoch, about one million years ago, horses which would be acknowledged as such today were grazing the prairie and tundra.

By a curious coincidence of evolution, man appeared almost simultaneously, though he then had no inkling of the comradeship that was to flourish between himself and his partner in mounted warfare. By the early part of the Pleistocene epoch our primitive ancestor had descended from the trees, learned to walk on his hind legs, and discovered that sharpened flints, stones and sticks made useful tools and weapons. He had shed most of his natural hairy coat and ape-like appearance, and his brain was capable of some intelligent reasoning and thought-processes.

It is a remarkable fact that, soon after the appearance of the horse proper in America, he became extinct in that continent—perhaps as a result of a devastating epidemic like the dreaded horse sickness of South Africa. Thus, although the United States can claim to be the birthplace of the world's horse family, no human being set eyes on the animal in North America until AD 1519, when Hernan Cortés astonished and confounded the Aztecs of Mexico with his troop of centaur-like cavalrymen.

It seems certain that the horse's first acquaintance with his future master was not altogether a happy one. To *Equus*, this strange creature, erect on two legs, was yet another dangerous predator that used its dangling front paws to hurl fearsome missiles at him. To *Homo*, the timid beast that would not defend itself was another source of a good dinner. Sad evidence of man's early use of his second oldest servant has been found in many Stone Age sites, specifically at Solutré in the Saône-et-Loire district of France, where a vast dump containing thousands of discarded horse bones was discovered.

No one can be certain how long it took our ancestors to realise that, if horse-steak made a tasty meal, the living animal also had its uses. All we can say is that man had domesticated the horse at some date —or more likely, at various dates—between 4000 and 2000 BC, and perhaps the first to do so were the nomad tribes of Central Asia known as Aryans. It is probable that these wandering herdsmen used the horse, like their cattle, as a source of flesh and milk; the drinking of fermented mare's milk, or *kumiss*, is practised by some Central Asian peoples, notably the Mongolians, to this day.

What did these 'Aryan' horses look like? Here at least, we can be more exact,

for living specimens of one type can still be seen. In 1881 Colonel N. M. Przevalski of the Imperial Russian Army was exploring in Mongolia when he came upon herds of wild pony-like beasts, specimens of which he took back to Russia. These were proved to be the original Asiatic wild horses and are regarded as the ancestors of many later breeds. In memory of their discoverer the animal has ever since been known as the Przevalski horse—a name which confounds most non-Russians and which is made more confusing by some reference works attempting to imitate the pronunciation by spelling it 'Prjevalsky' or 'Przhevalsky'. The animal can be seen in various European and American zoos; Prague has the largest herd. Standing about 12 or 13 hands, this primitive horse is a somewhat donkey-like beast, with a coarse head, thick neck and short, erect mane. He is usually dun in colour, and has narrow 'coffin' feet, like the ass.

There was another 'northern' type of wild horse, contemporary with the original Przevalski, which roamed the tundra of East Europe and Siberia. This was similar in appearance, but had a finer head and a dark dorsal stripe. Specimens of this European wild horse, or 'tarpan', have

Rameses II in action with his chariot corps, probably against the Hittites, c 1200 BC. The horses may be stylised, but their carriage and obvious breeding are typical of those of other contemporary artwork. This is a drawing from the sculptures in the Temple of Rameses also survived and captive herds are still bred in Poland.

The next development was to exert a profound influence on the course of warfare, and thus on world history: the horse became a riding and draught animal. Basing their assumptions on early drawings of chariots, some historians believe its first use was as a draught animal, but archaeological evidence suggests that man bestrode a horse before, or at least at the same time as, he harnessed him in draught. The earliest record of horse-drawn chariots—as opposed to bullock- or ass-drawn—dates from the Hittite empire of *c* 2000–1200 BC.

It is not difficult to imagine how man first came to sit on a horse. Herdsmen shepherding their cattle from pasture to pasture would quickly get the idea of saving their legs by scrambling up on some docile, plodding ox. But the sharply ridged bovine back is not adapted to receiving one of the tenderest portions of our anatomy, and what more natural than that, sooner or later, it should dawn on our early cowboy that the broad rounded back of a fat mare was less painful?

Whether the horse was first ridden or driven, it had to await the advent of the war-chariot to raise it above the common herd of domestic cattle and set the seal of nobility on its status. The chariot began as a primitive form of cart on wooden 'barrel top' wheels, drawn by oxen or asses. This clumsy vehicle was no weapon of war; it was too heavy and unwieldy for rapid manoeuvre. But somewhere in Mesopotamia, perhaps in the vast Hittite empire, someone evolved a Mark II version, of 2 or sometimes 3 horse-power. It was much more lightly built, with weight-saving spoked wheels, while its equine power unit gave it a performance that was far superior, both in speed and handling, than its crude predecessor. The arrival of the horsed chariot in the field

was a shattering development in contemporary warfare. Now, a commander was able to deploy a devastating form of mobile fire-power—the prototype of all fighting vehicles—and the effect on unprepared infantry was probably greater than that created by the lumbering British tanks on the Western Front in 1916. Squadrons of these vehicles bearing down with thunder of hooves, their archers spewing forth showers of arrows, must have been a terrible spectacle to face.

No written records survive to tell us anything about the war horses who 'powered' these early fighting vehicles, and when we refer to contemporary drawings, bas-reliefs and the like we should remember that artists down to recent times have been notorious for indulging in much licence when portraying the horse. Assyrian and Egyptian drawings mostly have one feature in common: they show very small animals by today's standards, apparently no higher than 14 hands; and, moreover, types which appear to be very well bred. They have lean, 'hot-blooded' heads well set on, with proud carriage, clean fine legs, short (if hollow) backs, and often a general appearance remarkably reminiscent of the pure-bred Arabian. The first war horses may well have been of Arabian origin, for it is maintained that all the 'hot-blooded' breeds stemmed from what was originally Arabia Felix, some 5,000 years ago.

From driving the horse into battle the next logical step was to ride him against the foe. The soldier mounted on a fleet, handy horse not only presented a difficult target for the spearman or archer, but having delivered his attack he could quickly withdraw if circumstances made it prudent to do so—always provided his horse was not a casualty. If his side were victorious, he could press the pursuit with more flexible mobility than the chariots

which, if not entirely confined to tracks, could only cope with reasonably good terrain.

Thus, starting somewhere around 900 BC, the first cavalry horses appear in the ranks of Assyrian, Scythian, Median and other conquering hosts from the Middle Eastern lands. At first they carried bowmen, who were expected to handle their weapons from the back of a galloping horse, with no saddle and no stirrups, as effectively as their comrades in the chariot corps. That they evidently did so is a tribute to their horsemanship. The harassing tactics of those mounted archers from Parthia became so well known that they have added a phrase to Western languages. Thundering up to bowshot range they would loose off a volley, wheel their horses about and, twisting round, send a 'Parthian shot' dead astern as they galloped out of range of spear and javelin. Eventually the archer was superseded by the mounted spearman, or lancer, but it is doubtful whether he could have effectively used his weapon for thrusting; without

Assyrian archers of the time of Assurbanipal. From a relief in the Palace of Nineveh, *c* 639 BC. The 'Number Two' feeds the bowman with ammunition

saddle or stirrups the shock of impact would surely have been sufficient to topple him over his horse's croup. Most likely, he hurled it at close quarters, and then drew his short sword for the in-fighting.

Until 1929 our ideas of these Asiatic war horses were derived chiefly from artists' conceptions. But in that year the Soviet archaeologist Dr S. I. Rudenko excavated a complex of burial mounds of the fifth century BC in the Altai mountains of Western Mongolia, near Pazyryk. This was a momentous event for, whereas all previous digs had yielded only skeletal remains, here by an extraordinary climatic accident the tombs had been engulfed in ice shortly after the interment, with the result that all the contents were perfectly preserved in a natural deep-freeze. Among them were the bodies of sixty-nine horses, all so remarkably intact that not only were the external features almost lifelike, but the internal organs and even stomach contents showed little decomposition. These horses were broadly classified into two main types. The first was obviously a blood animal standing from 14.3 to 15 hands, with the 'Arab-type' head of concave profile, short back and clean legs with good bone; the prevailing colour being a golden dun, with black, unhogged mane and long tail. The other group were the 'common' draught horses (harness was found), with rather coarse heads, short legs and long backs. The stomach contents showed evidence of grain feeding, while the presence of geldings as well as entires and mares indicated that some form of selective breeding was practised.

The custom of burying a chieftain's horses along with his body and worldly goods was a funerary rite observed by ancient warlike tribes down to classical times; it may well have been the origin of a custom which can be seen today when the charger of some departed general, or monarch, is led behind the funeral gun-carriage, boots reversed in the stirrups.

From about the same date comes one of the earliest descriptions of a war horse—and the most oft-quoted biblical reference to it:

Hast thou given the horse strength? Hast thou clothed his neck with thunder? Canst thou make him afraid as a grasshopper? The glory of his nostrils is terrible. He paweth in the valley, and rejoiceth in his strength: he goeth on to meet the armed men. He mocketh at fear, and is not affrighted; neither turneth he back from the sword. The quiver rattleth against him, the glittering spear and the shield. He swalloweth the ground with fierceness and rage: neither believeth he that it is the sound of the trumpet. He saith among the trumpets, Ha, ha; and he smelleth the battle afar off, the thunder of the captains, and the shouting.

(Job 39 : 19–25)

Dating from about 400 BC, the above passage is a remarkable piece of imagery which immediately conjures up the romanticised vision of the proud, mettlesome war horse perpetuated by artists and poets ever since. And when King James I's translators put it into English for the Authorised Version they produced a fanfare of prose which rings with the sonority of cavalry trumpets. They also made utter nonsense of much of the original. A curious beast this, with his thunder-clad neck! And what are we to make of those gloriously terrible nostrils? If he is as timid as a grasshopper, how does he mock at fear? In the original Hebrew the term for 'thunder' was exactly the same as that for a horse's mane, while 'to be afraid' could also mean 'to start, bound or leap', and 'nostrils' should read 'snorting'. Those Royal Commission translators, in their superior wisdom, chose to employ the less likely variants. The anomalies were corrected in the first Revised Version (1885): 'Has thou clothed his neck with the quivering mane? Hast thou made him to leap as a locust? The glory of his snorting is terrible . . .' Not so striking perhaps, but at least credible.

When the Israelites were driven out of Egypt, *c* 1230 BC, they had no horses, and for some centuries afterwards, with hateful memories of the Pharaohs' chariots and horsemen, they regarded the animal as a beast fit only for pagan foes. The psalmist scorns the war horse: 'An horse is a vain thing for safety, neither shall he deliver any by his great strength', and the early books of the Old Testament are full of disdainful references. Moreover, it was a standing order that all horses captured were to be 'houghed'—'hocked', or hamstrung—though it would surely have been simpler, and more humane, to pole-axe them. Throughout his service to man, the horse has been subjected to a variety of suffering and torture, but hamstringing was surely one of the cruellest. The horse's hock corresponds to the human ankle, and hamstringing meant severing the powerful Achilles tendon, so effectively immobilising him. Thus mutilated, he could only adopt a painful squatting posture under searing sun and swarming flies—until he collapsed, and the vultures and jackals closed in. It is difficult to understand why the Chosen People should have inflicted such a barbarous, lingering death on their dumb captives. Human prisoners were despatched quickly and mercifully.

By the time King Solomon took over the throne from his father, David (974 BC), and astonished the Queen of Sheba with his might, the Israeli forces could deploy a formidable mounted arm; according to the chronicler, Solomon boasted of 40,000 'stalls' of horses for his chariots and 12,000 cavalry—no doubt many of the chariots would be needed for his harem of 700 wives and 300 concubines. The horses were grain-fed, forage supplies being properly organised: 'Barley also and straw for the horses and swift steeds brought they unto the place where the officers were, every man according to his charge' (I Kings 4 : 28).

The armies of the early Pharaohs were exclusively of infantry. About 1700 BC came the first of successive invaders coveting the fertile Nile Valley. These were the Hyksos, or 'Shepherd Kings', a shadowy people of whom little is known, except that they were probably nomadic Semites—and that they overran the Egyptians with that terrible fighting vehicle, the horsed chariot. If one cannot better the enemy's weapon, one copies it; and, with the rise of the Egyptian New Empire (1550 BC), the chariot corps, like the cavalry of later European powers, had become the élite of the regular army. According to contemporary artists, these early Egyptian war horses were small—14

hands at the most—and well bred with beautiful 'dish-faced' heads and fine, clean legs. Occasionally a painting or inscription will show a horseman among the charging chariot squadrons, but it is clear that he is not a cavalryman—possibly a mounted orderly? (Cf. motor cycle despatch riders in the early days of mechanisation). Cavalry as such came with the later Pharaohs, perhaps around 600 BC, and like that of the central Asian tribes was chiefly composed of mounted archers, though lancers or mounted spearmen and javelin-men were included.

Thus in ancient Egypt the pattern of the war horse's evolution was repeated: first the chariot animal, then the troop horse. Some authorities suggest that the chariot horse was too small and light to be of use under a warrior, and therefore a heavier type was deliberately evolved by selective breeding; but contemporary art does not bear out this theory. Down to the time of Alexander, and after, artists and sculptors continue to depict the same little 'breedy' animals with their Arab-type heads. And, as the history of the Arabian itself shows, there seems no reason why these pretty 'picture book' horses should not have served in the mounted squadrons; the warring Bedouin's horse rarely stood more than about 14.2 hands until after he was brought to Europe and the USA at the close of the last century.

By 530 BC the vast empire of the Persians under Cyrus the Great had straddled the Middle East from Bactria to Egypt, and the war horse had played an important role in its conquests. Herodotus tells us that the armoured Persian horsemen and their death-dealing chariots were invincible: 'no man dared face them'. According to Xenophon, the Persians had no horse-soldiers before the Cyrus empire, only chariots (and infantry), and so the credit for the famed and feared Persian cavalry must be given to the great 'King of Babylon'. It is believed that the Persians inherited their mounts from Bactria (part of the present northern Afghanistan) via the conquered Medes. When the Greeks encountered them they called them Nisaean horses, after one of their legendary heroes—implying an obvious compliment to their breeding and performance. Even as late as AD 211 these Persian horses were being extolled by the Greek poet Oppian in his *Cynegetica*—one of the earliest extant treatises on hunting: 'The horses of Nisaaea are the handsomest, fit only for mighty rulers. They are splendid, running swiftly under the rider, obeying the bridle willingly . . .'

By the third century BC the Chinese emperors maintained powerful mounted forces to shield their Great Wall against the constant Hun marauders from the outer space of Mongolia. Their tactics were copied from the barbarians themselves, and their horses were the same type of shaggy Mongolian pony of 12 or 13 hands—direct descendants, no doubt, of the original Asiatic wild horse, or Przevalski's. Just as later great powers strove to outdo their rivals with bigger guns and better tanks, the Sons of Heaven sought to improve their cavalry's horseflesh. In 128 BC, intelligence reported a source of superior remounts in Bactria, near the modern Samarkand, and an Imperial trade mission was despatched thither, eventually returning with a score of 'heavenly blood-sweating stallions'. These were surely of the same Nisaean breed admired by the Greeks in Persia, and they formed the nucleus of Chinese military stud farms which, by the seventh century AD, boasted more than 300,000 breeding animals. Not only did these horses enable the Chinese to overcome their barbaric neighbours once and for all, but they were to have a significant effect on European history. Pushed ever westwards

by the Imperial cavalry squadrons, the Huns spewed forth into the Occident, and were only prevented from over-running the whole of Europe when Attila was humbled by the Roman might in the field of Catalaunia in AD 451.

Our knowledge of ancient horsemanship is sketchy to say the least, being inferred chiefly from contemporary art, and it is only when we reach classical Greece that any clear picture emerges of how the horse was schooled, ridden and managed, for war and peace.

During nearly twenty-three centuries the name Xenophon has been familiar to horsemen as well as classicists, for around 360 BC he wrote what are now the earliest extant treatises on horsemanship and cavalry training: *Hippike* and *Hippicarchakos*, usually rendered in English as 'On the Art of Horsemanship' and 'Duties of a Cavalry Commander'. Though he was a cavalryman of every rank from troop leader to general, Xenophon unfortunately tells us little about the actual employment of the horse on the battlefield, nor does he mention anything about the breeds employed during his time, even if he has plenty to say on desirable points to look for when selecting a mount. Nonetheless, our knowledge of the contemporary war horse, and his rider, would be infinitely the poorer without his works.

The best-known representations of Greek war horses are those proud creatures on the Parthenon frieze, showing off their 'parade' paces in a procession, or review. Since this work was executed by the great artist Phidias about 440 BC—that is, only ten years before Xenophon was born—we might expect them to be typical of his time. And when Xenophon's description of the ideal horse is compared with some of those on the frieze, there is much similarity. All stallions, they are compact, well coupled, with fine legs and heads; some carry their heads rather over-bent

Horses of Xenophon's time showing off their 'Parade' paces on the Parthenon frieze (*c* 440 BC)

at the poll in the then admired fashion, while others are 'star-gazing', but this may have been an artistic device to avoid a monotonous effect. Xenophon nowhere mentions size, but judging by their riders these animals are no more than 14 hands or so. However, there is a theory that the Parthenon frieze, as seen at eye-level, gives a misleading impression. The frieze was originally erected more than 35ft above the ground, and was intended to be viewed from directly underneath, thus altering the perspective. The horses are a useful weight-carrying type, certainly heavier than those dainty creatures that drew the Egyptian chariots, and perhaps the sort one might today expect to result from an Arab-cob cross.

The perfect troop horse, says Xenophon, should be 'sound-footed, gentle (ie not vicious), sufficiently fleet, ready and able to undergo fatigue, and first and foremost, obedient'. A disobedient horse was not only useless, 'but he often plays

15

the part of a very traitor'. A curious point is his insistence on the use of a muzzle whenever a horse is handled without his bridle, 'to keep him from mischievous designs'. The Greeks, like all the ancient peoples, rode only stallions in war—as the artists were at pains to make clear—and stud-owners today are well aware that entires are prone to indulge in playful, or not-so-playful, nips. While the war horse had to be capable of jumping ditches, walls and banks, it is odd that the Greeks did not use artificial, 'made' obstacles; all training was carried out over natural ground. Xenophon makes no reference to riding schools or *manèges*; on parade, the horse should be balanced and collected, so that he carries himself in a 'graceful and striking manner' and this is not to be achieved by jerking his mouth or kicking him in the belly:

> Most people think that this is the way to make him look fine; but they only produce an exactly contrary effect— they positively blind their horses by jerking the mouth up instead of allowing them to see where they are going, and by spurring and whipping, frighten them into confusion so that they run headlong into danger. This is the way horses behave that are fretted into ugly and ungraceful action. But if you teach your horse to go with a light hand on the bit, yet to carry his neck high and bend his head, you will make him do exactly what he himself delights in . . .

The Greeks did not shine as cavalrymen until after Xenophon's day; it was Philip of Macedon who organised the Greek cavalry into a formidable fighting arm, and it was his son Alexander the Great who proved them in battle. No one will dispute that Alexander's conquests and the final overthrow of the King of Kings, Darius, were owed largely to the horse;

his four great victories, from Granicus to the Hydaspes, were gained by his brilliant handling of the mounted arm which he employed to deliver the decisive stroke at the crucial moment. The battle of Issus (333 BC), in which Darius lost 110,000 men and Alexander a mere 450, was fought near the modern Iskanderum (Alexandretta) in Syria. Some 2,200 years afterwards the last great cavalry campaign in history reached its triumphant conclusion only a couple of days' march away, when Allenby's Desert Mounted Corps shattered the remnants of the Ottoman Empire.

With Alexander, comes one of the most celebrated war horses of all time, and among the first on written record; what is known of Bucephalus is derived from Greek and Roman authors, all of whom wrote centuries after Alexander's charger met his death in India. Thus there are many conflicting details: he is described variously as black, bay, chestnut, even skewbald; veritably, a horse of many colours! Even the derivation of his name is in doubt: the Greek word *Bucephalus* means 'ox-head', and according to some writers he was so named because he had a large star and blaze suggesting the shape of an ox's head with horns. When Marco Polo travelled through Badakhshan (now a province of Northern Afghanistan) in 1260, the locals 'asserted that not long since there were still found in this province horses of the breed of Alexander's celebrated Bucephalus, which were all foaled with a particular mark on the forehead'— a pretty story, but one dismissed as pure myth by modern historians.

The currently accepted view is that Bucephalus was one of a well-known breed of Thessalian horses which were distinguished by a head with an exceptionally broad, prominent forehead and wide poll, rather like that of the ox. These were common in Greece and Macedonia long before Alexander's time; they are described by Aristophanes, and appear in many sculptures and other art works. Typical examples are the famous head by Phidias, from the Parthenon, and a bronze in the Uffizi Gallery in Florence.

The story of Alexander's acquisition of Bucephalus is related by Plutarch and Pliny, and has been repeated, with embellishments, down the ages. King Philip bought him from a Thessalian gentleman for 13 talents (16, according to Pliny)—an astonishing and doubtless exaggerated figure equalling some £7,000 today. It was a rash deal, for the king had not even tried him until he was brought to the royal stables, where he proved ill-tempered and unmanageable, and would allow no one to mount him. Resigned to cutting his losses, Philip ordered the groom to take the useless brute away. But Alexander—then a boy of twelve—begged his father to let him try.

The king turned on his presumptuous son: 'Boy, do you boast of greater knowledge than your elders and betters? Do you think you are more skilled in horsemanship than any of these?'

Retorted the boy: 'I can manage that horse better than they do'.

'So! And what will you forfeit for your rashness if you fail?'

'The price of the horse, sire!'

Amid taunting laughter Alexander went up to Bucephalus, made much of him, and quietly turned his head to the sun. Apparently, the others had not noticed that the highly-strung animal was upset by his own shadow dancing before him. Without fuss or bother, Alexander was soon on the horse's broad back, and to the amazement of the assembled crowd trotted him quietly round the courtyard and out

Detail from the Pompei mosaic of Alexander the Great, showing his horse's head

The Roman cavalry as seen on the Trojan
Columns, Rome. It is doubtful whether horses
could have survived much work in this casing
of leather scale-armour

into the open parkland, where he in-
dulged in a gallop. Philip and the on-
lookers were dumbfounded. 'My son,'
cried the king, 'You must seek out a
kingdom worthy of you; Macedonia is
not broad enough for you.'

Bucephalus was no colt when purchased, as some writers assert; he was
fourteen years old. We can only wonder
that he had survived to this age if 'unmanageable and vicious'—which leads us
to suspect that Plutarch *et al* were indulging in a little *de mortuis* flattery of a
national hero when they related the above
incident. But there is no doubt that
Bucephalus became Alexander's first charger, and at the ripe age of twenty-three he
crossed the Hellespont with the expeditionary force that was to conquer half the
known world. As a first charger he was
not ridden on the line of march, but,
except at the battle of Granicus (where
possibly he was lame?), Alexander always

called for him when action was imminent: 'So long as he was engaged in drawing up his men, or riding about to give orders, or to review them, he spared Bucephalus, who was now growing old, and made use of another horse; but when he was actually to fight, he sent for him again, and as soon as he was mounted, commenced the attack.' (Plutarch, *Lives*).

Alexander's final triumph was the defeat of the Indian king Porus at the battle of the Hydaspes (River Jhelum, Punjab), in 327 BC. His noble charger was now at least thirty years old, but he bore him, as usual, into the thick of the fighting; Alexander emerged unscathed, but Bucephalus was sorely wounded by spear and javelin in neck and flanks—'Though at the point of death, and almost drained of blood, he turned, carried the king from the very midst of the foe and then and there fell down, breathing his last tranquilly now that his master was safe'.

The king was distraught at the loss of his faithful friend, and Bucephalus was said to have been buried with full military honours at the spot where the Greek forces had crossed the Hydaspes river. Then Alexander ordered a city to be built on the site, which he named Boukephala. According to Plutarch, this became one of the most important of the conqueror's many foundations; but, if the story is true, the name soon vanished from history, and nothing like it has survived in the neighbourhood.

The relationship between Bucephalus and his royal master is unusual in Greek annals. It is clear that the Greeks did not normally show much affection for their horses; they regarded them not as friends and companions, but purely as servants, for use only in war and hunting. They did not ride for pleasure, and nowhere in their literature is there any suggestion of friendship between man and mount—with the solitary exception of Alexander and Bucephalus. When, during the eastern campaign, the conqueror reached the Caspian (Hyrcania of the Greeks), some bandits ambushed his grooms and carried off Bucephalus. Whereupon Alexander issued a proclamation threatening death to every man, woman and child in the district unless the horse was returned unharmed. He was speedily recovered.

Like the Greeks, the Romans did not at first take kindly to the horse, which they regarded as a beast fit only for barbarian marauders. The strength of the Roman empire lay in its stolid infantry of the legions who, like the British redcoats of Marlborough and Wellington, formed the backbone of her armed might. At the time of the Emperor Augustus the war establishment of the Roman army was twenty-five legions, each of 5,300 all ranks; the mounted arm consisted of a single squadron, 120 strong, attached to each legion and employed not for shock action but merely for reconnaissance and escort duties. Later, having reluctantly learned the lesson from their foes, the Romans came to appreciate the value of a flexible, swift-moving arm that could deal decisive hammer blows at the crux of an infantry fight, and the cavalry were organised into what we should term corps and divisional troops, available for deployment by the field commander when and where required. The regiment was the *Ala*, of 500 officers and men (though a few were 1,000 strong), divided into troops of about thirty-two men each—an organisation remarkably similar to that of cavalry regiments within living memory. There was no Roman Xenophon to record any details of their horses and horsemanship, but, according to Tacitus, all the European cavalry were mounted on horses from Spain, said to be of Numidian origin —a small, hardy breed which had contributed greatly to Hannibal's defeat of the Romans. There were Gallic and German horses, too: 'slow and ugly', observes Tacitus, and probably descended from the original 'cold-blooded' wild horse of Europe. Evidently the troop horses were unusually well 'corned', for Polybius, in his detailed description of the Roman army (c 120 BC), says that the monthly ration was 10½ bushels of barley per horse, which works out at the remarkable figure of about 20lb a day. In the last days of horsed cavalry the usual ration was 10–12 lb of oats, or about 10lb of barley—and this for a much heavier animal.

One of the very few descriptions of a typical war horse by a Latin writer is that of Virgil in his *Georgics* (c 30 BC):

His neck is carried erect; his head is small; his belly short; his back broad. Brawny muscles swell upon his noble chest. A bright bay or a good grey is the best colour; the worst is white or dun. If from afar the clash of arms be heard, he knows not how to stand still; his ears prick up, his limbs quiver; and snorting, he rolls the collected fire under his nostrils. And his mane is thick, and reposes tossed back on his right shoulder. A double spine runs along to his loins.

Much of this smacks of Job's passage, with which doubtless Virgil was familiar. By 'double spine' he means a backbone which is sunken between the muscle and flesh on each side of it—the most comfortable seat for the human posterior with no saddle.

If the above animal seems a paragon, then the charger which Julius Caesar is alleged to have ridden must have been a startling freak. According to his early biographer, Gaius Suetonius (second century), 'Julius Caesar rode a horse with remarkable feet nearly like those of humans; his hoofs being split after the manner of fingers, etc.' Since the primeval four-toed ancestor of the horse had become extinct many millions of years before Caesar's charger was foaled, this story might be dismissed as a piece of fanciful myth—yet, there could be some truth in it. Remarkably enough, there are well-documented cases of such extraordinary reversions to original type. In his classic *Points of the Horse*, Captain H. M. Hayes gives a photograph of an English mare with a well-formed second 'toe' on the off fore leg, and adds 'we occasionally find in the horse that one or both of the (vestigial) splint bones are provided, like the cannon bone, with a more or less perfect pastern and hoof. In fact, there have been well-authenticated instances of horses which were so completely furnished in this respect that instead of being shod on only four hoofs, they carried iron on eight' (three shoes on each forefoot, one on hind). With the present-day cost of shoeing, horsemen may be thankful that such freaks are rare.

When Caesar led his first abortive expeditionary force to Britain in 55 BC he landed without any cavalry support, for his transport ships were blown off course and failed to make the assembly point. It could be said that the fate of this early 'Operation Sealion' was decided by the horse. As is made clear in Caesar's own report, *The War in Gaul*, the Celtic barbarians made devastating use of their mounted arm, against which the invaders were helpless. On the very beaches the chariots and cavalry—'a class of warriors of whom it is their practice to employ in battles'—met the legionaries struggling through the surf with such intrepid boldness and vigour that the first wave was beaten back, and only the timely arrival of reinforcements made a landing possible. Even when a bridgehead was established, Caesar's lack of cavalry prevented him from fully exploiting the success. Whenever he moved, the enemy horsemen and

ET SAPIENTER: AD PRE LIVM:

William of Normandy's cavalry, as depicted on the Bayeux Tapestry

chariots were upon him, pouring hails of spears and arrows into the dismayed infantrymen and then galloping out of range. In the end, the expedition was forced to withdraw across the Channel.

The lesson was well learned by Caesar; for his second, victorious, invasion the following year, he assembled a force of five legions supported by 2,000 cavalry from Gaul, the latter riding their heavy breed of 15-hand horses. Though the British mounted troops fought as boldly as before, they did not choose to confront the heavy cavalry of the invaders face to face, but relied on harassing tactics which were no more than a thorn in the flesh to the overpowering might of the steel walls of the legions.

The horses used to such good effect by our Celtic ancestors were really no more than 13-hand ponies—from which, it is said, some of the present British mountain and moorland breeds are descended, notably the Shetland, Exmoor and Welsh. After the final Roman withdrawal from Britain no more is heard of the war horse until the Norman Conquest. Certainly, the successive waves of Danish, Norwegian and Saxon invaders brought horses with them and breeding was encouraged, but not, apparently, for military purposes. The Saxons, like the early Romans, were not cavalry-minded, even though they venerated the horse itself as a cult symbol, and used it for hunting and transport. The first Saxon chieftains to set foot in Britain were those two brothers Hengist and Horsa, whose names have a peculiar significance: Hengist is an anglicised variant of the modern German *Hengst* 'stallion', while Horsa has obvious connections with the English 'horse'. When King Alfred defeated the Danes, he managed it without the aid of the horse— a fact which did not greatly concern him, for the Danes were also infantrymen by choice. And, if Alfred laid the foundations of the British navy, he also did much to found a good stock of horses for his royal stud. He imported stallions, and imposed laws regulating the breeding and export of animals. He appointed a 'Horse Thegn', a high court official equivalent to the later Master of the Horse. Yet, with all this activity in the horse world, and despite the rising interest in horse racing, the Saxons obstinately declined to mount a horse for battle, putting their trust firmly in the infantry fyrds, as their predecessors had done in the legions.

Horses
Great and
Small

Fourteenth-century knights in action. Complete
body armour for horses had not yet been
adopted

The Saxons' curious disregard of the horseman as a weapon of war was to prove their downfall. When William of Normandy confronted Harold at Hastings in 1066 his principal striking force was a body of about 1,000 heavy cavalry, supported by archers and infantry. The Saxons had no mounted arm, and the king himself led his army on foot. At first Harold's infantry fyrd and his élite Huscarles (guards) fought gallantly and effectively; with their terrible 5ft Danish battle-axes, they repulsed the thundering waves of armoured knights, 'lopping off arms and striking off horses' heads at a single stroke'. Believing the enemy were routed, they broke their formation and streamed in pursuit. This was the cavalryman's opportunity, and William seized it. Leading the reserve himself, he hurled his squadrons upon the disorganised infantrymen, smote them down and sent them reeling back. The close-support fire of the archers eventually finished the day. As Oman observes, 'the tactics of the phalanx of axemen had been decisively beaten by William's combination of archers and cavalry'.

The Norman Conquest saw the introduction of the fully-armoured knight to Britain—and, it is sometimes said, of the 'great horse', or *destrier*, which was to command the battlefields of Europe until the invention of firearms ousted his supremacy. But William's troop horses and chargers were by no means the heavy, 16-hand type that the medieval knights bestrode. The Bayeux Tapestry, executed only a few years after the Battle of Hastings, provides the most detailed contemporary evidence, with more than two hundred pictures of horses, and clearly shows a much lighter and smaller animal. Though all the figures are obviously much stylised, the horses seem to be little more than about 14 hands, for the riders' legs hang far below the girths and, when hit,

the animals bowl head over heels, indicating that they could charge at a pretty pace. The ponderous 'great horse' of the medieval knight could manage nothing swifter than a lumbering trot. And these Norman cavalrymen had little need for a heavy animal, for their armour was light chainmail, thin scales of metal sewn on to leather tunics. Like the ancient warriors, they rode only stallions—a detail which the tapestry seamstresses were no doubt tickled to emphasise.

William had two chargers, black Spanish horses, presented to him by Duke Alfonso of Spain; these animals were of the excellent Andalusian breed, then and long after esteemed throughout Europe. William and his successors did much to improve the horse in Britain; when not fighting they were hunting, and the horse was an essential adjunct to both pastimes. Spanish, French and Flemish sires were brought over, and gradually larger and heavier types of animal evolved to complement the changing pattern of mounted warfare.

By the twelfth century the aristocratic order of knighthood, or chivalry, had spread its influence throughout Europe. Drawn exclusively from the nobility and 'county' families, the élite ranks of the mounted knights were everywhere regarded as the flower of military might, while their code of conduct in war and peace came to symbolise the highest ideals of human behaviour. On the battlefield, the knight and his horse reigned supreme; they had become the *raison d'être* of armies, and the humble serfs and peasants of the infantry were regarded as little more than a necessary nuisance. As Oman records in *The Art of War in the Middle Ages*:

Foot soldiers accompanied the army for no better purpose than to perform the menial duties of the camp, or to assist in the numerous sieges of the period. Occasionally they were employed as light troops, to open the battle by their ineffective demonstrations. There was, however, no important part for them to play. Indeed, their lords were sometimes affronted if they presumed to delay too long the opening of the cavalry charges, and ended the skirmishing by riding into and over their wretched followers.

Although, in Xenophon's Greece, the cavalry had been a corps d'élite, it exerted no lasting influence. It was the unchallenged supremacy of the knightly man-at-arms of medieval Europe that set the seal on the superiority of the horseman; even though he eventually lost his operational importance, it is the cavalry regiments, whether horsed or mechanised, which have ever since been accorded precedence over every other arm in the world's fighting forces. From the war horse and his rider came the very word 'chivalry', and all it stands for; *chevalier*, *ritter*, *caballero* have their origins in the 'noble' animal.

The history of warfare is one of a constant struggle between conflicting tactical desiderata: mobility, firepower, and protection. The Norman knights on their small, handy mounts enjoyed both mobility and striking power, for their light armour was adequate protection against contemporary weapons—except, perhaps, those Danish battle-axes. Then came the crossbow, deadly at close range; and shortly afterwards the Anglo-Welsh archers were to prove that the queen of medieval weapons, the longbow with its clothyard shaft, could bring down an armoured horseman almost before he had time to urge his mount into an earth-shaking charge. Lacking any form of close-support artillery to counter these new weapons, the horseman could only resort to better protection—hence the develop-

ment of plate armour. To carry this extra weight, he needed a much more powerful mount, and so the 'great horse' was evolved. This was not a specific breed, but a type, embracing stock from the Low Countries, France and the Lombardy Plains. His leading characteristics were his size and massive build. Standing up to 17 hands, he was the personification of equine power: short-coupled, with deep barrel; Roman-nosed, 'cold-blooded' head; thick, heavily-feathered legs and immense quarters—whence, perhaps, the expression 'a bottom like a Flanders mare'. His likeness can be seen today in the English Shire Horse and the Percheron.

Destrier, the correct name for the 'great horse', is a Norman–French word derived from *dextrarius*, right-handed. Some writers maintain the horse was so called because it was always led by the squire or groom off his right hand, but there is nothing peculiar in this; dismounted horsemen have always walked on the near side of their animals, with reins or halter rope in the right hand. Another theory is that 'right handed' signified superior strength, or pre-eminence; man is normally stronger in the right hand than the left, and from time immemorial the right flank ('right of the line') has been the place of honour in a formed body of troops.

Early writers on horsemanship claimed that some of the spectacular 'airs above the ground' performed in classical equitation originated in the defensive, or offensive, actions taught to the knight's charger. For instance, in a mêlée a sudden *capriole*—flying leap with hind legs lashing out—would effectively remove all assailants from the immediate vicinity. But it is quite obvious that the 'great horse' was utterly incapable of any such gymnastics; it was as much as his rider could do to spur him into a sedate trot. In fact, there is no evidence that any of the medieval war horses were ever schooled to perform such 'airs' for battle purposes. Artists have traditionally portrayed mounted monarchs and generals in such attitudes as the *levade* or *croupade*, but this was merely a flattering convention. If a charger reared or lashed out in battle, it was usually without any bidding from his master, who was probably just as disconcerted as his attackers.

The 'great horse' had become great indeed; when his own carcass of body armour was buckled on and his iron-encased master had been hoisted into the heavy structure of iron, timber and quilting that was the saddle, with weapons, housings and accoutrements, the horse was burdened with some 30 stone (420lb or 224kg)—10 stone more than the 15–16 hand troop horse of the twentieth century, in full marching order, was expected to carry.

So ponderous was the 'great horse' that he practically defeated his own object. He lacked manœuvrability; he could not be ridden on the line of march, and the vast quantities of forage required for his enormous frame must have caused severe headaches among contemporary quartermasters. Across country, he was liable to become bogged down. At Bannockburn, for instance, Edward II's knights were nearly all 'ditched' in a muddy stream behind which Robert the Bruce had taken up position.

The knell of the heavy war horse was sounded at Crècy (1346), when the English archers laid low the flower of French chivalry. Lacking nothing in courage, the squadrons of some 2,500 knights and men-at-arms put in sixteen distinct charges, but always with the same result. Hissing in at ever-shortening range, the storms of arrows brought the horses crashing down, bristling with shafts like giant hedgehogs and effectively impeding the following ranks. No horseman could come within striking distance of the bowmen; by nightfall 1,542 'men of gentle blood'—and undoubtedly many more horses—were dead on the field, for the loss of a mere handful of fifty English. Never again did the French cavalry dare to face this terrible form of firepower. At Poitiers and Agincourt they dismounted their knights, with results that were even more disastrous; as Oman says, 'Middle-aged knights of stout habit and body died of heart failure in battle without having received a wound'.

It is best not to contemplate the image of a stricken *destrier* pierced with a dozen barbed shafts, each convulsive struggle forcing them deeper, and twisting them in his entrails. A *coup de grace* with an axe was the best he could hope for.

The horse had meanwhile been helping to fashion an empire's glory that was eventually to reach from the cradle of civilisation almost to the heart of Europe. Before the advent of Muhammad and the Islamic faith, the Arabs of Arabia Deserta were a scattered complex of idolatrous nomadic tribes, constantly at war amongst themselves. Remote in their harsh desert homeland, they were virtually unknown to the rest of the civilised world. By the time of Muhammad's death in AD 632 the whole of these fractious tribes had become fused into a single people whose simple tenet 'There is no God but God and Muhammad is his Prophet' became the foundation of one of the world's greatest faiths and was to lead them far beyond the Arabian peninsula.

Although the Arabs used camels on the march and for pack transport, they owed their physical mobility essentially to the horse—and they produced an animal which, in war and peace, has exerted a profound influence on nearly all other breeds. Within the last 200 years only one breed has rivalled it; and the Thorough-

Mounted mêlée at the Battle of Crècy

bred owes many of its characteristics to its Arabian forebears.

The question of when the Bedouin started breeding and riding horses is bound up with the origin of the Arabian horse itself. Some 'pro-Arabian' enthusiasts and breeders, such as the late Lady Wentworth, who wrote voluminously on the subject, claim that the Arabian was a unique, distinct breed originating in Arabia itself several thousand years before the Bedouin were united by Muhammad. According to the opposing faction, this is nonsense: Arabia was always an arid, waterless desert, entirely unsuitable for the large-scale breeding of horses, and the early geographers and historians make no mention of the horse in their writings. They quote Strabo (63 BC–AD 20) who asserts categorically that there were no horses in Arabia in his time. Some of them claim that the breed originated in North Africa, an off-shoot, perhaps, of the Barb or Numidian type, and only arrived in Arabia after Muhammad's day.

Recent archaeological and geological research seems to support the 'Arabian' school of thought. Evidence suggests that Arabia was not always Arabia Deserta, but, like the Sahara, was once fertile, with flowing rivers, forests and pasture. Figures of warriors and hunters on horseback have been discovered in rock inscriptions in both north and south Arabia, dating back to about 1000 BC, thus disproving the much-quoted statement of Strabo, who never visited the country himself. The remarkably Arab-like heads of those ancient Egyptian and Assyrian chariot horses, quite distinct from the North African breeds, have led many to believe that these were in fact of pure Arabian blood. The pre-Islamic literature of the Arabs contains abundant references to the war horse, which leave no doubt that it was as prized then as in the days of the great conquests:

The grey mare, the renowned, in the
  world there is none like her,
Not with the Persian kings, the
  Chosroes, the Irani,
Spare is her head and lean, her ears
  pricked close together;
Her forelock is a net, her forehead a
  lamp lighted
Illuminising the tribe; her neck curved
  like a palm branch,
Her withers clean and sharp. Her
  forelegs are twin lances,
Her hoofs fly forward faster ever than
  flies the whirlwind,
Her tail-bone held aloft, yet the hairs
  sweep the sand . . .
      (Tufeyl al Kheyl, *c* AD 500)

Lo, the mares we bestride at the dawn
  of battle!
Sleek coat mares, the choice ones;

ourselves have reared them.
Charge they mail-clad together, how
  red with battle,
Red the knots of their reins as dyed
  with blood.
Are not these the inheritance of our
  fathers?
Shall we not to our sons in turn
  bequeath them?
      (Amr bin Kulthum, *c* AD 530)

The above translations are taken from Lady Wentworth's *Authentic Arabian Horse*.

Much of the controversial mystique surrounding the origin of the Arabian horse stems from the mythical Bedouin traditions and the legends of the early poets. These were deliberately fostered by Muhammad who, though no horseman himself, quickly recognised the value of the horse as a weapon of war. His earliest great battle with the opposing Meccans at Mount Uhud in AD 624 resulted in his resounding defeat by superior mounted forces. From then on he built up his cavalry arm and actively encouraged the breeding of horses by all possible means, including religious exhortation. The faithful were assured that Allah's own hand was upon the horse: 'The Evil One dare not enter into a tent in which a pure-bred horse is kept . . . every night an angel comes down to each horse, kisses the hair of his forelock and asks Allah's blessing on him'. Good horsemastership was to be rewarded in Heaven: 'As many grains of barley as thou givest thy horse, so many sins shall be forgiven thee'.

It is doubtful whether the Bedouin needed such encouragement, for they had been devoted horsemen long before Muhammad set the seal of holy approval on their 'drinkers of the wind'. For centuries they had cherished the tradition that the 'One God' had bestowed upon them the pure-bred Arabian horse.

Then Allah took a handful of the South Wind and He breathed thereon, creating the horse and saying: 'Thy name shall be Arabian, and virtue bound into the hair of thy forelock, and plunder on thy back. I have preferred thee above all beasts of burden, inasmuch as I have made thy master thy friend. I have given thee the power of flight without wings, be it in onslaught or retreat. I will set men on thy back that shall honour and praise me, and sing Halleluja to My name'.

While this shows that from the earliest days the dwellers in the black tents had esteemed the horse as a noble beast of war, the reference to the special friendly relationship between master and mount is interesting. For generations Westerners were fed with sentimental stories about the Arab's unique love for his steed. The horse, it seemed, was treated like a pet dog, living with the family in the tent, feeding from his master's hand, singling him out from a multitude with joyful whinnies of recognition. The loss of a favourite mare was mourned by a warring sheikh more deeply than the death of one of his wives. William Palgrave, who travelled in Arabia in 1856, brought back similar tales of the Arab's alleged devotion to his horse, but could not help classing 'these pretty stories' with many other mythical legends of the desert.

One of those best qualified to comment on these stories was Lady Wentworth's mother, Lady Anne Blunt, who with her husband, Wilfrid Scawen Blunt, made extensive tours of Arabia in the 1870s, studying the Bedouin and their horses. Later they founded the first Arabian horse stud in Britain at Crabbet Park. In her books *A Pilgrimage to Nejd* and *The Bedouin Tribes of the Euphrates*, Lady Blunt makes it clear that although the tribesman prized a fine mare for her value as a weapon of

war, there was little element of affection in his admiration, and his conception of 'horsemastership' ranged from callous indifference to brutality.

The Bedouin's land was cruel, his life harsh; only the fittest could survive, and there was bred in him a fatalistic outlook on life and death. All suffering and misfortune was the will of Allah. Thus indifferent to his own wellbeing, it is small wonder if he may have disregarded that of his horse. As Lady Blunt wrote:

The desert-bred horse had everything against him from the first. Starved before birth he is generally a puny foal, but is nevertheless weaned at a month . . . even during the first month he is not allowed to run with his dam, being kept at the tent ropes . . . nor has he any exercise unless the tribe be on the march. Then in his first autumn, he is turned out to shift for himself, shackled to prevent him being stolen . . .

Lady Wentworth adds that the wounded mare unable to keep up with the marching tribe was relentlessly left behind to die of thirst, 'while the evil carrion birds circle overhead'. When Charles Doughty, another nineteenth-century traveller in Arabia, asked why a suffering mare was not mercifully despatched with a gunshot, the Bedouin were shocked; whether the animal lived or died was Allah's will alone.

The Arabs were unique among early mounted warriors in riding only mares; colt foals were not welcome, and only a few were reserved for stud purposes. This preference is reflected in the common Arabic word for 'horse': *faras*, the basic meaning of which is 'mare' (conversely the English word 'horse' originally implied 'stallion'—as it still does among some country folk, notably in Wales). Gelding was not practised by the Arabs until modern times, being considered an affront to the nobility of the species—though the same high principle was not, of course, applied to the human male, who had his uses as a eunuch.

For many centuries there were two schools of thought about the question of stallion versus mare as a cavalry mount. The Arabs, with some justification, held that the entire is likely to betray a stealthy approach or recce patrol by whinnying lustily the moment he scents an interesting female, and that he is apt to bite not only his equine rivals but his master as well. On the other hand, the 'pro-stallion' school maintained that the mare, like the female of other species, tends to be temperamental and unreliable, especially when in season, and lacks the courage, stamina and showy bearing of the proud-stepping stallion. Possibly some psychological influence may have been at work, too. War is a man's business: the battlefield is no place for the 'weaker sex', whose prime duty is to produce offspring. This controversy continued down to the late nineteenth century, when there was much debate about mounting some of the British Indian cavalry regiments on stallions only.

The hosts that followed the green banners of Islam to central Asia, the Mediterranean and the bastions of Europe in the seventh century were essentially light cavalry. The small pure-bred desert horse—never higher than 14.2 hands—was the ideal mount. It was light and active, with no surplus flesh and, mare or no, possessed the undisputed staying power and courage that distinguish the Arabian breed today. Armed with bows and lances, the Arabs would make a sudden eagle swoop on an enemy's flank or marching column, and then a swift withdrawal. Except for the dismounted archers, such infantry as was scraped together was little more than an ill-armed, unenthusiastic rabble, useful only for camp chores. In 732, exactly a century after the Prophet's death, the all-conquering *Jihad* reached its climax when the armies of the believers burst through the Pyrenees and carried fire and sword across France as far as the Loire valley. It was the horse that had crowned their triumph, but it was the despised infantryman who proved their *ne plus ultra*. At the Battle of Tours, turning point in European history, the stolid Frankish soldiers of Charles Martel presented an unbreachable wall, 'standing as a belt of ice frozen together and not to be dissolved'. The light Arab horsemen could make not a dent, and when their great leader, Abd-al-Rahman, was slain, they melted away.

Western armies again met the Arabian war horse when the Seljuk Turks—or Saracens—spewed forth from their Central Asian frontiers and captured the Holy Places of Palestine. Although vast numbers of cavalry were employed on both sides during the Crusades, there were no great cavalry engagements; the campaigning was chiefly one wearisome siege after another. Riding short on their handy Arabs, the Saracens employed the usual Muslim tactics of harassment, and refused to become embroiled in head-on collision with the armoured knights.

It is popularly thought that the latter were mounted on the massive *destrier* of European battlefields, but much more credible evidence points to a lighter stamp of animal, many of them Spanish—no doubt the Andalusian. It is unlikely that the ponderous mount of chivalry could have survived the ardours of desert warfare, even if he had plodded those 2,000-odd miles from France and England. As with other mounted campaigners in later times, replacement of horse casualties was a constant problem, and remounts were picked up from any convenient source, including the enemy. In 1100, Baldwin, crusader 'King' of Jerusalem, contracted to replace horses lost in action, which he did from local sources, but there was also an organised supply from Europe, which were given free passage to Syria.

Casualties among horses in battle were caused chiefly by the deadly arrows from the mounted Saracen archers, who would not come within range of lance or sword. The armoured knight was relatively immune from arrows—if not from the heat—but his mount was vulnerable, for horse-armour was scarcely practical in such a theatre of operations. At the disastrous battle of Mancura some 800 of 1,200 Frankish horses are said to have been slain by the archers. Possibly the early war correspondent may have included the wounded in this figure, for one animal staggered out of action with fifteen arrows sticking in him—and survived.

Although the Saracens, when in a tight corner, would hamstring their horses to deny them to the enemy, there are many stories about chivalrous commanders presenting some Christian knight with a charger as a mark of esteem for personal valour in battle. The Frankish or English knight was usually a bigger man than his Arab opponent, and more heavily armoured, but he greatly prized the hardy Arabian 'pony', finding to his surprise that it was equal to his weight. Saladin himself is supposed to have bestowed one on King Richard, and it is said that the Lion Heart was riding this same animal when he was treacherously captured in Austria on his way home.

One could say that the nations which today adhere to the Muslim faith from Malaysia to Morocco were founded in the hoofprints of the Arabian horse. No war horse in history has had such far-reaching influence on man's affairs and on horse breeding in general. In most of the world's prized riding horses flows some blood of the Arabian, whether he be Thoroughbred (or *Pur Sang* or *Vollblut*), American Saddlebred, Welsh pony, or the noble Lipizzaner of Vienna.

One of the Arabian's characteristics is his remarkably fine, dense bone structure, which enables his slender limbs to carry more weight than might be expected. In appearance and carriage, he has always been the perfect 'picture book' horse. His gazelle-like head with 'dished' profile (*Jibbah* as the Arabs term it); arched neck; fine, clean legs, and showy carriage have made him the exemplar for artists seeking to show equine beauty at its best.

Wheeling Squadrons

An Austro-Hungarian hussar
of 1748

In the early thirteenth century a tidal wave of mounted warriors burst out of the high plateaux of Central Asia and, sweeping all before it, ravaged the whole of the Middle East and pounded against the gates of Europe. The name Genghis Khan* has become synonymous with death and destruction; while his savage hordes have been likened to a devastating typhoon. However posterity may have judged him, there is no denying his brilliant genius as a cavalry general, and his troops were among the finest light horsemen the world has ever seen. The very antithesis of Muhammad, whose Islamic legacy he was to shatter, the Great Khan was a man of deeds, not words. Born an illiterate nomad of the cruel Gobi desert, he founded within his own lifetime an empire that stretched from the China Sea to the Baltic—some two-thirds of the then known world. His astonishing conquests were achieved entirely on the backs of the shaggy Mongolian ponies that were the direct descendants of the wild Przevalski horse.

For centuries before Genghis Khan's time the horse had been the fulcrum of the nomad's very existence; it defeated the limitations of vast distances, and made possible far-ranging pastoral movements and raids. Almost from birth, the Mongolian boy was brought up as a horseman. Before he could toddle, his first riding lessons were on the back of a sheep, and by the age of sixteen, when he was enlisted as a warrior, he was virtually living in the saddle. He ate and drank, even slept, on the back of a horse, and did not bother to dismount to answer the calls of nature. Sent on an errand of a few hundred yards, he would leap on the nearest pony rather than use his own legs. He was weaned on mares' milk and,

sheltering in his *yurt*, created some semblance of warmth by burning horse dung. When rations ran out on a forced march, he stuck a knife into a horse's vein, sucked a pint or so of blood and sewed up the wound. Sometimes the blood was stored in gut bags made from the horses' intestines; heated over a fire, this served as a sort of black pudding emergency ration. On the march, slabs of raw beef or mutton were rendered chewable by the simple process of clapping them on the horse's back underneath the saddle and riding on them.*

As a babe, the Mongolian was doused daily in cold water to toughen him up, thus effectively putting him off bodily hygiene for the rest of his life, for he seldom washed again. The trooper's garments were worn continuously, day and night, and only when they became threadbare were they renewed. He tore his greasy meat with his hands then wiped them on his boots, to keep the leather supple. Rancid butter was stored away in hairy pockets, and any unconsumed portions of the day's rations were stuffed down the rider's trousers and sat upon in the saddle. It was said that a Mongol army on the march could be scented by the enemy up to a distance of twenty miles, if the wind was right.

The all-conquering hordes were exclusively cavalry and the horse was their sole means of mobility. Bred to incredible hardship, the native Mongolian pony was not a handsome beast, but he was as tough as his rider. Standing about 13 hands, he had a coarse Roman-nosed head and a thickset deep-barrelled body with long mane and tail. His shaggy coat

* A practice common among other Asiatic nomads:
   . . . His countrymen the Huns
   Did stew their meat between their bums
   And the horses' backs whereon they straddle,
   And every man eats up his saddle.
            —Samuel Butler, *Hudibras*

* Also found as 'Jenghiz', but modern historians prefer the more accurate transliteration 'Chingis'.

was usually dun in colour—ideal as camouflage in his native environment—but bays, chestnuts and greys were not uncommon.

The stamina of these ponies is legendary yet they subsisted entirely on the sparse herbiage of the steppe, for the Mongols grew no cereals. Marches of 80 miles a day for days on end were nothing unusual for the advancing hordes; according to the unique *Secret History of the Mongols*, forced marches of 120 miles in one day—probably of 24 hours—were recorded. A man did not ride a single horse throughout; as one tired, he switched to a fresh mount, perhaps using ten or more in a day.

One might suppose that the herds of reserve horses would have created prob-

A mounted Mongol archer. The Mongolian pony may have been undersized and coarse, but his stamina was legendary

lems, but each group of these docile little beasts followed a bell-mare, which was either ridden or led in hand. When action was imminent, they were dropped behind with an escort. Sometimes superior numbers of the enemy might be overawed by the Mongolian ruse of mounting dummies on the spare horses. And the ponies had other uses: in the last resort, they served as emergency rations; unlike most other cavalrymen, the Mongol was not averse to eating his mount. With so many horses, casualties were less of a problem and, as grazing was always available, the vast self-sufficient mounted hosts could easily cover distances impossible for more conventional forces.

Marco Polo recorded that:

Their horses are fed upon grass alone, and do not require barley or other grain. The men are habituated to remain on horseback during two days and two nights, without dismounting; sleeping in that situation whilst their horses graze . . . Their horses are so well broken-in to quick changes of movement, that, upon the signal given, they instantly turn in every direction; and by these rapid manoeuvres many victories have been obtained.

The popular conception of a Mongol horde as a wild, undisciplined rabble riding hell-for-leather, with no command structure and little thought for horseflesh, seems far from the truth. In Genghis Khan's day the army was properly organised on a decimal system of units: a troop comprised ten men, a squadron ten troops, a regiment ten squadrons. At formation level was the division, or *touman*, of ten regiments—10,000 men, with perhaps 100,000 horses. A formidable command; and certainly no other army had ever fielded such a vast array of horse-flesh. Discipline was strict. The Khan's

The Great Khan attacks the Chinese

standing orders, quoted in the *Secret History*, laid down that any trooper disobeying an order was to be flogged and put under arrest, while those who failed to carry out a personal order from the Khan himself were to be beheaded on the spot. Good horsemastership was not overlooked: 'Take care of the spare horses in your troop before they loose condition. For once they have lost it, you may spare them as much as you will, they will never recover it on campaign'. On the march, the men were not to tire their horses by galloping about after game—an understandable temptation for these natural hunters—and the pace of the march was to be a steady jog-trot. Bridles were not to be worn: '. . . if this is done, the men cannot march at a gallop'—and no unauthorised personal baggage was to be carried on the saddle.

Chinese and Mongolian troops of Timur-i-Leng (Tamarlane) in mortal combat (fourteenth century). The lancers would seem more at home with the pitchfork

The tactics of the Mongol cavalry were similar to those of other mounted nomad peoples: lightning attacks on the flanks of an enemy, ambushes and feigned withdrawals. Often a horde would lure pursuers on for two or three days; then, mounting their spare horses, they would turn and deliver a ferocious assault on the exhausted enemy column. All planned attacks were preceded by thorough reconnaissance.

The main assault troops were the mounted archers armed with fearsome bows of 170-lb draw-weight,* with which they could pour in showers of arrows at full gallop. It is odd that, although the mounted bowman was an essential arm

* The maximum draw-weight of a modern composite tournament bow seldom exceeds 42lb; that of the English archers at Crècy was about 80lb.

of most Asiatic armies, he was never adopted in Europe. Perhaps the standard of horsemanship was not high enough, for handling a bow in the saddle obviously demands a secureness of seat and agility not easily acquired—and an unusually well-schooled horse. The swordsman and lancer needed only one hand to use his weapon, the other being free to control his mount—hence, the left has always been known as the 'bridle hand'—but in action the archer must drop his reins and rely on legs alone. Today in the Soviet Central Asian province of Kazakhstan a form of mounted archery is still popular—undoubtedly a legacy of Mongolian hordes.

Though the Mongol empire at its zenith reached across the greater part of the western hemisphere, these horseman-hordes left behind no enduring influence; they founded no great cities and bequeathed nothing to European or Oriental culture. But their horsemanship and light cavalry tactics have never been surpassed; and descendants of the gallant little Mongolian pony that assured them their victories are still to be seen, virtually unchanged, in their original homeland. Little was known about their actual training until the nineteenth century, when an explosion of Western interest in Central Asia, largely occasioned by the 'power game' between Russia and England, resulted in a procession of bold European travellers venturing into those inhospitable regions. For the first time since Marco Polo, accounts were brought back of the habits and customs of the primitive inhabitants, which had changed little since the days of Genghis Khan.

In 1876 Colonel Fred Burnaby, Royal Horse Guards, published his *Ride to Khiva*, the story of his remarkable adventures in Turkestan. His description of the Kirghiz nomads and their horses tallies very closely with what is known of their thirteenth-century predecessors:

No horses which I have ever seen are so hardy as these little animals which are indigenous to the Kirghiz steppes ... The Kirghiz never clothe their horses even in the coldest winter. They do not even take the trouble to water them, the snow eaten by the animals supplying this want. In fact, it is extraordinary how any of these animals manage to exist through the winter months, as the nomads hardly ever feed them with corn, trusting to the slight vegetation which exists beneath the snow ... But once the snow disappears and the rich vegetation which replaces it in the early spring comes up, the animals gain flesh and strength, and are capable of performing marches which many people in this country would deem impossible, a ride of a hundred miles not being at all an uncommon occurrence in Tartary. Kirghiz horses are not generally well shaped and cannot gallop very fast, but they can travel enormous distances without water, forage, or halting. When the natives wish to perform any very long journey they generally employ two horses; on one they carry a little water in a skin and some corn, whilst they ride the other, changing from time to time to ease the animals. It is said that a Kirghiz chief once galloped with a Cossack escort (with two horses per man) 200 miles in twenty-four hours.

Like the former hordes, the Kirghiz relished a horse-steak if all else failed and, unlike the Arabs, set no great store by their animals: 'The descendant of Ishmael will seldom sell his horses, no matter how much money you may offer ... The Tartars will sell everything they have for money'.

Burnaby's book provoked an anonymous letter to *The Field* in April 1877, which gave some little-known details of horse training among the Tartar tribes.

The training the best of them underwent for the business [of war] was something appalling, and to anyone unacquainted with the constitution and iron hardness of the Tartar ponies would be completely incredible. Their method of training a horse, or rather, the ordeal they made him pass through before he was considered suitable for the war path—which they admit used to kill two out of five who underwent it—was in this wise: After picking out a likely one, rising seven or eight—before which age no horse was allowed to be selected for raiding—they loaded him with a sack of earth or sand, at first only the weight of the rider, but gradually increased for eight days until the horse carried 20 or 22 stone. As the weight was increased, the ration of food and water was diminished. He was trotted and walked six or seven miles daily. Afterwards, for another eight days they gradually decreased the load, still, however, decreasing the feed until the sack was empty. Finally giving him for two or three days absolutely nothing at all, but merely tightening up the girths at intervals. About the nineteenth day they worked him hard until he sweated, when they unsaddled him and poured buckets of ice-cold water over him from head to tail. He was then picketed to a peg on the open steppe, allowed to graze, or fed sparingly ... This training was, of course, a sort of epitome of what the animals often had to undergo on an actual foray, when they had frequently to swim semi-frozen rivers, carry great weights, go for days without food, be picketed on the steppes sweating from a long journey, in snow and sleet, without any covering ...

Surely no other cavalry horses have ever been subjected to such draconian methods of training—and few could have survived it.

It is often claimed that the invention of firearms spelt the death of horsed cavalry. As a simplification this might be true, but the horse took an unconscionable time a-dying—in fact, some five hundred years. It is nearer the truth to say that the increasing preponderance of fire-power forced the cavalry to adopt and alter their tactics to the extent that they lost their status as the pre-eminent arm. In 1520 Machiavelli put the proud horseman firmly in his place when he wrote in his *Art of War*: 'It is right to have some cavalry to support and assist infantry, but not to look upon them as the main force of an army, for they are highly necessary to reconnoitre, to scour roads ... and to lay waste an enemy's county, and to cut off their convoys; but in the field battles which commonly decide the fate of nations, they are fitter to pursue an enemy that is routed and flying, than anything else'.

This brusque dismissal, which has probably delighted infantry-inclined historians ever since, was a remarkably accurate forecast of the mounted arm's principal role in future wars, even though the horseman obstinately continued to decide many great battles, down to Allenby's victories in Palestine in World War I.

If the art of warfare is reduced to elementary principles there are only two ways of defeating an enemy in the field: he can be attacked, with cavalry or infantry, and overwhelmed in close combat, or he can be driven back by an impenetrable hail of missiles, without coming to grips. While, of course, both methods may be used in a variety of combinations, the history of war shows a see-saw of alternating shock action and missile ascendancy.

Up to medieval times the charging horseman was supreme and the 'villainous saltpetre' was slow to have any real effect upon him. The first cannon appeared during the early years of the fourteenth century—Edward III is said to have used a few at Crecy—but they were cumbersome, unpredictable in performance and often as much a hazard to their own side as to the enemy. The first hand-gun was the equally clumsy arquebus of the fifteenth century, which was ineffective above about 80 yards and took nearly one minute to send off a single erratic round. The English archer with his long-bow could loose off up to ten arrows a minute, deadly at 250 yards, and a company of bowmen could put down a storm of missiles into a 'beaten zone' through which no man or horse could penetrate. The main disadvantage of the arquebus and its lighter successor, the matchlock musket, was its crude method of firing: a piece of smouldering tow, or 'match', was applied to the priming powder in the touch-hole— a system which, surprisingly enough, lingered on in artillery weapons until well into the nineteenth century.

A step forward was the wheel-lock musket of the sixteenth century, in which a revolving wheel struck sparks from a piece of pyrites held in the cock, and finally, about 1650, came the flint-lock. Here the spark was produced by the falling cock striking its flint against a piece of steel over the pan—a much more certain and quicker process. With slight modifications the flint-lock reigned supreme for nearly two hundred years, and its finest development was seen in the famous 'Brown Bess' musket which helped Wellington's squares to hurl back the French horsemen at Waterloo.

Though the range of the early musket was limited, it was sufficient to prevent the swordsman or lancer from charging to within striking distance; and so, on the principle 'of if you can't beat them, join them', the cavalryman took to firearms as well. In sixteenth-century Europe, and up to the Civil Wars in England, he became little more than a mounted pistoleer; in an attack each rank trotted up to the enemy, fired their pistols and wheeled about to the rear to reload. Very often they were more anxious to wheel about than to advance within effective range. Shock action was forgotten, and a century or more passed before it dawned on cavalry leaders that such tactics sacrificed the sole advantages of the horseman—mobility, and the momentum of a charging line. Moreover, the use of firearms on horseback is an uncertain business, particularly with an excitable mount that might choose to throw up his head at the moment of firing. In an attack of the French 3rd Cuirassiers during the Peninsular War an officer who had lost his sword drew his pistol and let fly. Horse and rider crashed to the ground, and when the officer picked himself up he found he had neatly blown off the top of his charger's head.

In Western Europe all through the seventeenth century and well into the next, cavalry remained 'heavy', mounted on large, slow-moving animals, and battle tactics were based chiefly on the use of the pistol rather than the *arme blanche*. During this period, too, many mounted troops ceased to be cavalry proper. The French introduced the dragoon, who was armed and fought as a foot soldier, merely using his underbred cob as a means of transport. As the worthy Dr Johnson observed in his *Dictionary of The English Language*, the term 'dragoon' denoted 'a kind of soldier that serves indifferently either on foot or on horseback'.

While the 'metropolitan' cavalry of civilised Europe were sinking into the doldrums, a type of light horseman was evolving among the more primitive peoples of the vast Hungarian plains, who was eventually to become the beau ideal of the dashing cavalryman of romance, and whose tactics were to influence the breeding of the war horse throughout the Continent. The original Hungarian hussar was very like his Mongolian prototype, virtually living on horseback and relying entirely on the mobility of his handy mount in battle. The early eighteenth-century French historian, Gabriel Daniel, gives some curious details of the contemporary hussar:

Their customary mode of fighting is to surround an enemy's squadron and affright it with their strange cries and queer movements. As they are very expert in managing their horses, which are small, and as they ride with very short stirrups and press the spurs close to the flanks, they force them to a greater speed than that of heavy cavalry . . . what makes their horses so nimble is that they are fitted only with bridoons; and thus they breathe more freely, and pasture at the shortest halt without unbridling. When they halt after a good run, the hussars rub their horses' ears and tails to revive their flagging spirits.

By 'bridoons' Daniel meant the simple snaffle bit as opposed to the numerous varieties of severe curb or curb-and-bridoon which the heavy cavalry horse had now to submit to; but, since a horse breathes entirely through his nose, it is difficult to imagine why this should have any effect on his wind. And though a horseman may often rub his tired mount's ears, tail rubbing is usually known only as a habit of the animal itself symptomatic of 'sweet itch' or parasites.

The Magyar horsemen with their *blitzkrieg* tactics soon became notorious throughout Europe, and their peculiar form of lightning attack unpreceded by any customary softening-up was dubbed the *coup d'hussard*. Little more than freebooter marauders at first, the hussars were later embodied in the Austro-Hungarian forces. Under Frederick the Great and his brilliant leaders, von Zieten and Seydlitz, the 'light cavalry spirit' reached its zenith and became the model for every other European army.

While the Western powers were busily breeding their heavy, big-boned horses for their cuirassiers and regiments of Horse, the Magyars were well content with their own tough, handy little 'ponies' which could out-march and out-gallop any opponent. According to the modern Hungarian authority, Jankovich, the medieval hussar rode a Tarpan type of beast, of about 13 to 14 hands, but in the course of time this was crossed with oriental importations and Arab blood again became predominant among the war horses of Europe. When the so-called 'Spanish' style of horsemanship (*a la brida*) became fashionable in the fifteenth century, the Magyars would have none of it. In 1480 King Ferdinand of Naples gratuitously despatched a 'Spanish' expert to the Hungarian royal court so that these barbarians might learn the true art of horsemanship. King Matthias promptly returned him with the curt message:

With the horses which we trained ourselves we defeated the Turks, subjected Siberia, and vanquished all before us, honorably by means of our own horses. We have no desire for horses that hop about with bent hocks in the Spanish fashion; we do not want them even as a pastime, still less for serious business.

In England after the demise of the fully-armoured knight, the Middle Ages saw a decline in the mounted arm—and consequently in horseflesh. Successive monarchs were at pains to improve the standard of horse breeding, chiefly with the war horse in view. The practice of allowing inferior stallions to run free was forbidden by edicts of Henry VII, which enacted that all entires should be kept stabled—hence the term 'stallion', or 'stalled one'. Naturally, this led to much inconvenience among stud owners, and thus gelding became common. It is evident that the general standard of size was considered too low for military purposes. Henry VIII decreed that no stallion under 15 hands and no mare under 13 hands should be allowed to run wild, and every Michaelmas local magistrates were to organise drives to round up and destroy not only such animals, but also 'all unlikely tits, whether mares or foals'. Though well intentioned, such laws had unfortunate repercussions, for they resulted in wholesale, indiscriminate slaughter of potentially good stock as well as the 'tits'. When, under the threat of the Spanish Armada, Elizabeth ordered a grand muster and review of all her troops at Tilbury in 1588, the country could produce only a miserable showing of 3,000 cavalry which, says Blundeville, were mounted on 'very indifferent, strong, heavy slow draught-horses, or light and weak'.

The previous year, a Venetian traveller, Giovanni Michele, had given his opinion of the English cavalry horse:

As to the cavalry [I speak of light cavalry]—if it were but a good description it might be very numerous as that island produces a greater number of horses than any other region of Europe; but the horses being weak and of bad wind, fed merely on grass, being like sheep and all other cattle kept in field or pasture at all seasons . . . they cannot stand much work, nor are they held in much account; but nevertheless as they are mettlesome and high couraged, more especially if they chance to be Welch, they are said to do fairly (according to their small strength) for reconnoitring and foraging, and to harass the enemy, and they would do much better were they fed better. With regard to heavy horses, good for men-at-arms, the island does not produce any, except a few in Wales and an equally small amount from the Crown stud; so the country cannot have any considerable quantity. The heavy horses, therefore, now seem all are foreign, imported from Flanders, the Queen having chosen all persons to provide the amount assigned them, lest from want of horses the thing should fall into disuse, as it was doing.

This report—which must have pleased Philip of Spain—shows that the idea of the 'great horse' and his knight still lingered on, although 'the thing' was virtually obsolete. The favourable references to Welsh stock are curious; although the native ponies and cobs of Wales have been justly admired for centuries, there is little evidence that they were ever used in battle. The Welsh people themselves, being chiefly hill folk, were not cavalry-minded, and it is difficult to imagine what those few 'heavy horses, good for men-at-arms' could have been, unless they were the ancestors of today's sturdy Welsh cob. The original species in Wales was the small mountain pony of some 12 hands, hardy and sure-footed, but scarcely suitable as a troop horse. When the Roman legions withdrew from Britain they left behind a small cavalry force which retired to the fastnesses of central Wales and eventually became naturalised. Many of their horses were of the famed Andalusian breed, and tradition has it that these were crossed with the mountain ponies to produce the heavier, weight-carrying cob.

Despite Michele's unflattering remarks, the English cavalryman and his mount were to prove decisive factors in the upheaval which cost King Charles I his head and the country its monarchy. After Prince Rupert had shown the devastating effect of true shock action at Edgehill, Cromwell quickly learned the lesson, and improved upon it; and the great battles of Marston Moor and Naseby, besides innumerable lesser actions and skirmishes, were decided by the cavalry.

While the Swedish soldier-monarch Gustavus Adolphus is usually credited with the reintroduction of shock action when he joined in the Thirty Years' War (1630), it was Prince Rupert who gave it its true impetus. Gustav's troopers were drilled to trot up to the enemy, fire a single volley with their pistols, and then, instead of retiring to reload, 'fall on' with the sword. At Edgehill, Rupert forbade the use of the pistol, ordering his men to ride home with the sword alone, and at full gallop. This was the cavalry charge proper, which was to become the ultimate dream of every cavalryman until his horse was superseded by the mechanical vehicle. But in the wild excitement of a charge, men no less than their mounts are liable to get out of hand, and strict discipline is needed over both if the attack is to be effective. The rally is as important as the charge. Rupert's madly elated squadrons could not be rallied at Edgehill; they vanished from the field to plunder, leaving the king's sore-pressed infantry bereft of any cavalry support.

Though then a humble, unknown Captain of Horse, Cromwell saw the mistake, and profited by it. Long before the New Model Army was raised in 1645, Cromwell's regiments and troops of Horse had become a model for all time. Rigid puritanical discipline, precision of drill and adequate horsemanship, combined with a deliberately fostered *esprit de corps* raised them far above the gallant but independent-minded and uncontrollable Royalist horsemen. As Sir John Fortescue remarks in his *History of the British Army*, 'for once it may be said that the English horse stood in advance of all Europe'.

Sir John is using the term 'horse' in a military sense, to denote mounted troops, but there is evidence to show that the animal itself must have been admirably suited to its job. Although the Thoroughbred had not yet been evolved, the English horse, as a type if not a breed, was taking shape. Gervase Markham, writing in *A Soldier's Accidence* (1617), claimed:

I do daily find in my experience that the virtue, goodness, boldness, swiftness and endurance of our true bred English horses is equal to any race of horses whatsoever ... The true English horse ... is of tall stature and large proportions; his head, though not so fine as either the Barbarie's or the Turks, yet is lean, long and well-fashioned; his crest is nice, only subject to thickness if he be stoned, but if he be gelded then it is firm and strong; his chyne [back] is straight and broad; and all his limbs large, lease, flat and excellently jointed. For their endurance I have seen them suffer and execute much and more than ever I noted of any foraine creation.

Allowing for some pardonable patriotism, this suggests that there must have been a remarkable improvement in English horse-breeding since Michele's report of only twenty-nine years earlier.

The English Civil Wars (1642–58) are particularly well documented with contemporary diaries, letters, memoirs and 'true accounts', from Cromwell and Clarendon down to humble troopers; but it is remarkable how little mention is made of the horse in any of these writings. When all men rode, both in peace and war, the animal, it seems, was taken very much for granted. Contemporary illustrations usually depict idealised types, and can hardly be relied upon; in Vandyke's painting, for instance, Cromwell is shown mounted on a 'great horse'. Certainly some senior commanders were well mounted on superior stamps of animal— Prince Rupert is known to have ridden a 'black Barbarie' at one period—but no details are given, though there are plenty of references to his faithful little dog, Boy, which followed him throughout the early campaigning until killed at Marston Moor.

In his *Horses and Saddlery*, Major Tylden relies on a monument to Sir Richard Astley in Patishull Church, near Wolverhampton, which depicts a number of troop horses:

The horses are of a type which one would expect from what has been said about them. All have long tails and manes laid on the off, small heads not markedly either coarse or Eastern type. They are short in front of the saddle, well coupled up with plenty of depth, and strong, rather short quarters. The officer is riding a stallion. They are definitely short and thick in the neck and are ... probably about 15 hands. They are entirely different from the big clumsy horses shown in Newcastle's book and in drawings of the early years of the century.

But, as Tylden observes, it is impossible to say how much artistic licence is employed.

In addition to the cavalry proper—or Horse, as it was then termed—much use was made of the dragoon or mounted infantryman, whose animal was a 'sturdie nagge', a hairy-legged cob of about 14 hands. It is quite evident that this was inferior to the cavalry troop horse, for there are several references to prices allowed for remounts. When the New Model Army was formed in 1645, the Horse was empowered to pay £7 10s for a remount, but the dragoons were allowed only £4.

Whatever types of horses were employed, there is plenty of evidence to show that they were fully up to the rigours of hard campaigning. In July 1643 Prince Maurice's command of 300 Horse marched more than 90 miles in just over two days, and then fought the notable cavalry action of Roundway Down. Not surprisingly, the horses were described as being 'very tired'. Between 11 and 20 March 1642 Cromwell rode with five troops of Horse from Cambridge to Lowestoft, where he fought a general action and captured the town, and then returned to Cambridge, having covered rather more than 250 miles.

One of the most vivid pictures of a mounted encounter, and its consequence for the horse, is given in the journal of Captain Richard Atkyns, of Prince Maurice's regiment.* He describes how he nearly captured Sir Arthur Hazelrigg, of the 'Lobster' cuirassiers, at Roundway Down:

Twas my fortune in a direct line to charge their general of horse ... he discharged his carbine first, but at a distance not to hurt us, and afterwards one of his pistols, before I came up to him, and missed with both: I then immediately struck into him, and touched him before I discharged mine ... When he wheeled off. I pursued him ... and in six score yards I came up to him and discharged the other pistol at him, and I'm sure I hit his

head for I touched it before I gave fire ... but he was too well armed for a pistol bullet to do him any hurt, having a coat of mail over his arms and a headpiece. After I had slackened my pace a little he was gone 20 yards from me, riding three-quarters speed and down the side of a hill ... waving his sword on the right and left hand of his horse. I came up to him again (having a very swift horse that Cornet Washnage gave me) and stuck by him a good while, and tried him from head to saddle, and could not penetrate him, nor do him any hurt. But in this attempt he cut my horse's nose, that you might put your finger in the wound, and gave me such a blow on the inside of my arm amongst the veins that I could hardly hold my sword; he went on as before, and I slackened my pace again, and found my horse drop blood, and not so bold as before; but about eight score more I got up to him again, thinking to have pulled him off his horse. But he ... struck my horse upon the cheek, and cut off half the headstall of my bridle, but falling off from him I ran his horse into the body and resolved to attempt nothing further than to kill his horse; all this time we were together hand to fist. In this nick of time up came Mr Holmes to my assistance, and went up to him with great resolution ... whilst he charged him, I employed myself in killing his horse, and ran him into in several places, and upon the faltering of his horse, his headpiece opened and ... I had run him through the head if my horse had not stumbled ... By this time his horse began to be faint with bleeding, and fell off from his rate, at which said Sir Arthur 'what good will it do you to kill a poor man?' Said I 'Take quarter then.'

* *Journal of the Society for Army Historical Research* XXXV, 142 (June 1957).

Atkyns did not complete his capture,

for just then up came a Parliamentary troop who charged and rescued their general. Sir Arthur's horse 'dies on the spot'—as well the poor brute might, being pierced by numerous sword thrusts. According to Atkyns, it had been one of 'the late king's' (presumably James I) best animals which he rode at the mews. After the action Atkyns found that his own horse's bleeding had stopped, 'his cuts being upon the gristly part of his nose, and the cheek near the bone'. He ordered his groom to tend his wounds and bed him down well, but the rogue callously abandoned the animal with a farmer at Marlborough, 'and sold another barb of mine at Oxon, and carried my port manteau with him into the North which had all my clothes and linen in it . . . and I never saw him more'.

The reference to 'barb' suggests that not only the great commanders had superior horseflesh, but as the terms 'Barb' and 'Turk' were used very loosely to signify any Eastern breed it is not certain whether they were true Barbs, from North Africa, or Arabians. James I had encouraged the importation of oriental breeds—he is said to have been the first to import a pure-bred Arabian—and by the time the Civil War erupted, Eastern blood was common. That gallant Parliamentary cavalryman, Sir Thomas Fairfax, is stated to have ridden a Barb throughout his campaigning.

John Cruso says nothing about the types of horses required for the cavalry in his *Militarie Instructions for the Cavall'rie according to the Moderne Wars*, published in 1632. One of the earliest 'manuals' on training and horsemanship to appear in England, it was reissued at the height of the Civil War; the book must have enjoyed some currency and probably reflected contemporary thinking. Cruso was a Royalist, who is alleged to have been entrusted with the raising and training of cavalry in

Norfolk, but there is no evidence that he ever saw active service or was noted as a practical horseman. The illustrations in his book show the usual stylised, cavorting beast like the 'great horse' which was certainly not in fashion at that period. However, he does convey some idea of what was demanded of the animal in the field, and how he was supposed to be schooled for the service:

Concerning the horse (presupposing him to be of sufficient stature and strength, nimble of joynts, and sure of foot etc.) he must (of necessitie) be made fit for service, so as you may have him ready at command to pace, trot, gallop, or runne in full careere; also to advance, stop, retire, and turn readily to either hand . . . now, to bring him to this readie turning, he is to be ridden the ring, and figure 8, first in a great compasse, and so in a lesse by degrees, first upon his pace, then on the trot, and so the gallop and careere. These things he may be taught by using the hand, leg and voice. For the hand (observing not to move the arm, but only the wrist) if you would have him face to the left, a little motion of the little finger on that rein, and a touch of the left [sic] leg without using the spurre doth it: if to face (or turn) to the left about, a harder, etc. If you would have him trot, you are to move both your legges a little forward; for the gallop, to move them more forward, and for the careere to yerk them most forward, and to move the body a little forward with it . . . It were not amisse, after every thing well done, to give him some bread or grasse as a reward. For the voice, you may use the words Advance, hold, turn, or the like, but because the voice cannot always be heard, it were good to use him chiefly to the motions of the hand and leg. It will also be very useful to teach him to go sidewayes: this he may be brought unto by laying his provender somewhat farre from him in the manger, and keeping him from turning his head towards it. He must also be used to the smell of gunpowder, the sight of fire and armour, and the hearing of shot, drummes, and trumpets, etc., but by degrees, with discretion. When he is at his oats (at a good distance from him) a little powder may be fired, and so nearer to him, by degrees. So may a pistoll be fired some distance off, and so nearer ... It will be very useful sometimes to cause a musketeer to stand at a convenient distance, and both of you to give fire upon each other, and there-upon to ride up close to him: also to ride him against a compleat armour, so set upon a stake, that he may over-throw it, and trample it under his feet: that so (and by such other means) your horse (finding that he receiveth no hurt) may become bold to approach any object. He may also be used to mountainous and uneven wayes, and be exercised to leap, swimme, and the like ...

Some of these precepts would cause raised eyebrows among modern horse-men: 'yerking the legs most forward' would be as disconcerting to mount as to man. The directions for leaping and swimming seem oddly in advance of their time; it was not until well into the nine-teenth century that any serious attention was given to such training of the British cavalry horse. When, in 1756, a captain of the 10th Light Dragoons was so bold as to exercise his troop in swimming the River Thames and 'leaping obstacles', the phenomenon was judged remarkable enough to be reported in the press. Cruso's reference to the gaits of the horse is con-fusing. 'Pace' means the walk; for 'gallop'

read 'canter', and for 'careere', 'gallop'; in French the term *galop*, or *petit galop*, is used for the canter. The troop horse was never taught to 'pace'—an unnatural gait in which the animal moves like a camel, advancing both legs on one side simul-taneously; pacing was in use with the palfrey of the medieval knight and his lady, but not with the war horse. All horsemen, and particularly cavalrymen, would agree that it is useful to teach a horse to 'go sidewayes'. The half-pass is a recognised dressage movement, while the full pass—sometimes confusingly termed the *passage*, which is also applied to an-other quite different dressage movement— was very necessary to close the ranks on parade. Cruso's ingenious suggestion for teaching this movement seems curiously naive, and one wonders whether his con-temporary riders ever bothered much with the leg aid.

David Morier's picture of a private of the 8th Dragoons (later 8th Hussars) shows the typically 'cobby' dragoon mount with the docked 'Cadogan' tail

Bridled and Saddled

When the early nomad hunter first scrambled on to the back of a wild pony he was no doubt well pleased with himself if he eventually managed to stay aloft, to persuade his mount to advance roughly in the desired direction at the desired pace, and perhaps most important, to stop when required. He was now a rider, but he had a long way to go before he became a horseman. Obviously, if a soldier is to exploit the fullest use of the mobility provided by the horse, it is desirable that the animal should at all times be under his complete control—more especially so on the battlefield. As Xenophon remarked: 'It is plain that in moments of danger the master gives his own life into the keeping of his horse ... To sum it all up, the least troublesome and the most serviceable to his rider in the wars would be the horse that is, first and foremost, obedient'.

It is a far cry from Ancient Greece to the modern dressage arena, but the horse himself has changed little, and the elementary principles of riding him re-

Bridle, bits and saddlery of the mid-eighteenth century. The cheek-pieces were often 15in long, exerting severe leverage on the animal's mouth. This picture is from de la Guerinière's *Ecole de Cavalerie* (1733)

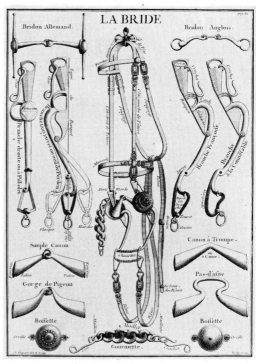

main. With no more than a pair of legs and hands, and some form of control over the horse's head, the rider can induce him to perform any desired movements, from the basic walk, trot and gallop to the most spectacular 'airs' of *haute école*. Today a serious student of equitation will maintain that no horse can be truly obedient without 'collection'. Put very simply, this term means that the horse is carrying himself in such a way that he has the maximum control over body and limbs. He is moving (or standing) 'at attention'; his simple mind is not distracted by the usual equine thoughts of food, or demons in the hedgerow, but is ready to respond instantly to the signals, or 'aids', transmitted via his rider's legs and hands. The classical French term *rassembler* is a perfect definition, for the collected horse is 'gathered together' between legs and hands.

It is doubtful whether any concept of collection was appreciated by primitive riders; even Xenophon could not have had much idea of it, for in all his writings he omits to emphasise the use of the legs,

without which true collection is impossible. Perhaps this is why those Parthenon stallions are either over-bent or 'star-gazing'. However, on the battlefield as opposed to the classical riding manège, the finer ideals of equitation were neither essential nor practical; it was enough if the horse would obey the simplest aids.

Whether those ancient mounted archers were horsemen or merely riders is debatable, but there is no doubt about their astonishing expertise on horseback. The Assyrian archer had neither saddle nor stirrups; at full gallop on his barebacked mount he could drop his reins, pluck an arrow from the quiver over his shoulder, nock it, draw the powerful bow to chin, and loose off a rain of missiles around an arc of nearly 300 degrees—all the while keeping his mount on course by legs alone. With the superseding of the mounted archer by the swordsman and lancer, such feats were not emulated again until the North American Indian took to the horse, perhaps 2,000 years later.

Saddles and stirrups are really non-essentials to the mere riding of a horse. Of much more importance is some form of bridle, and this is the oldest piece of horse accoutrement known to us. The most primitive form, notably used by the Numidians of North Africa, was simply a rawhide halter and rope, supplemented by a stick. Later it was realised that greater control was possible if the rope passed through the animal's mouth, and this became the prototype of all bits. It is, of course, quite possible to obtain adequate control over a horse without using a bit, and many modern horsemen, even in the showjumping ring, prefer a bitless bridle, which acts by pressure of the noseband on the more sensitive lower part of the horse's nose. But through the ages most riders, and particularly soldiers, have felt the need for something more positive; accordingly the animal's mouth has been

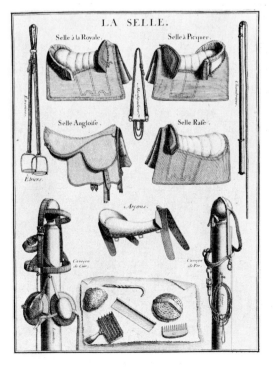

LA SELLE.

assaulted with an astonishing variety of ironmongery, some of it mild in action, some veritable instruments of torture.

The simplest form of bit still in common use is the plain snaffle, which is essentially a metal bar, or mouthpiece, lying over the tongue and resting on the toothless areas of gum conveniently placed between incisors and molars. Confusingly, perhaps, these are also known as the 'bars' of the mouth—not to be confused with the 'bars' of the foot! This elemental type of bit is the earliest so far discovered. Both plain and jointed snaffles were in use from about 1400 BC with the warriors of Assyria, Egypt and Scythia; but there is evidence that the type originated among the nomad horsemen of Central Asia. The Pazyryk excavations in Western Mongolia yielded perfect examples of a type now sold in saddlers' shops as the Jointed Full Spoon Snaffle.

The snaffle bit acts chiefly on the corners of the horse's mouth, its main effect being to cause him to raise his head. Since the Greeks used only the snaffle, this is probably one of the reasons why so many of their horses appear to be 'poking their noses'. In recent years, dressage riders have shown that it is perfectly feasible for a horse to be properly collected, with head flexed at the poll, using only the simple snaffle. But this demands considerable schooling of the animal and much expertise on the rider's part, including educated use of the legs. Early horsemen were not bothered about collection; to obtain greater control— and, possibly, the admired head-carriage —they took the easy way out and evolved the curb bit.

Like the snaffle, the curb bit is essentially a metal mouthpiece resting on the bars of the mouth, but an important addition is a length of chain (earlier, a piece of rawhide or rope) attached to each shank, or cheekpiece, of the bit and fitting under the horse's jaw in the chin groove. Tension on the reins causes the curb-chain to act like the fulcrum of a lever: it limits the backward movement of the cheekpieces and so transfers pressure on to the bars of the horse's mouth. The original theory was that, seeking to avoid this pressure, he will lower his head and flex his jaw, and if the discomfort is repeated, will slacken his pace. It is not known who first thought of this 'lever-action' curb bit; no doubt the simple expedient of using a piece of thong to act as a curb is as old as the bit itself, but such material perishes, and the earliest curb bits proper, with metal chains, are said to have been employed by the Iberian Celts of the fourth century AD. The idea spread and, by about AD 1000, the curb bit was in common use throughout Europe.

With the breeding of bigger, more powerful horses, it was considered necessary to have even greater means of control, and by the seventeenth century a truly frightening armoury of mechanical devices had been evolved, some of which if used today would probably result in prosecutions for cruelty. Enormous, curved cheekpieces nearly 15in long exerted almost enough leverage to dislocate the jaw with little effort on the rider's part (the cheekpieces of the last regulation pattern British Army bit were just over 4in long); a very high port, or arch, in the mouthpiece not only ensured that the bit pressed fairly and squarely on the sensitive bars, but it could severely bruise the palate. If this were not enough, some bits were fortified with deep serrations, and even spikes.

The early 'classical' works on horsemanship give the impression that the noble animal must have suffered more from the hands of his master in peace than from those of the enemy in war:

The nappy horse should be kept locked

in a stable for forty days, thereupon to be mounted wearing large spurs and a strong whip; or else the rider will carry an iron bar, three or four feet long and ending in three well-sharpened hooks, and if the horse refuses to go forward he will dig one of these hooks into the horse's quarters and draw him forward . . . an assistant may apply a heated iron bar under the tail while the rider drives the spurs in with all available strength.

Those words of wisdom were written by one Laurentius Rusius in his treatise entitled *Hippiatrica Sive Marescalia*, first published in Paris in 1533, and, astonishingly, still being reprinted nearly 200 years later. Until Xenophon's precepts of gentle coercion and reward were 'discovered' by such enlightened horsemen as de Pluvinel (1550–1620) and de la Guérinière (1688–1751), the wretched horse, whether for war or peace, was regarded as an obstinate beast, to be subdued primarily by brute force and punishment, rather than as a highly sensitive creature whose confidence must be won. Happily the unfortunate English term 'breaking'—for backing and schooling—no longer retains its original meaning.

Varieties of both curb bit and snaffle have remained in use, basically unaltered, to this day, but the curb was preferred for the more serious forms of horsemanship, that is, for military purposes, and in the High School manège. King Charles I, a horseman of some accomplishment, went so far as to issue an edict in 1627 forbidding the use of the snaffle except 'in times of disport', ie the chase; the cavalryman was to use only the curb.

The next development in bitting was what is now known among English-speaking peoples as the double bridle, or Weymouth: a curb and snaffle (or bridoon) used together, each with its own pair of reins. The theory here is that the snaffle raises the head, while the curb causes the desired bending at the poll. Until recent years this combination was regarded as a *sine qua non* for the well turned-out foxhunter, and for nearly a century was the regulation military bit.

During the early part of the nineteenth century it was firmly believed that the 'key' to an individual horse's mouth lay not so much in the rider's hands as in the bit; consequently a plethora of ingenious designs appeared. In 1832 the commandant of the Cavalry Riding Establishment at Canterbury aroused consternation among the ordnance department by recommending that each squadron of 100 horses should be equipped with no fewer than 105 different bits, including '45 for hard mouths; 25 for good mouths; 8 for very tender mouths; 12 for star-gazers and 10 for borers'. Fortunately for regimental quartermasters, the colonel's suggestions met with no enthusiasm from the War Office.

Towards the end of the last century the Weymouth, or double bridle, was rivalled by the variety now termed the Pelham: a single curb bit, but with two pairs of reins, which was supposed to combine the effects of the double bridle with the advantage of only one mouthpiece. Though still popular, and still the regulation type of bit in most surviving mounted units, including police forces, many horsemen question its practical efficiency.

Having discovered how to achieve some degree of control over his animal, the early horseman next began to ponder the question of greater comfort and security when mounted. The first logical advance was a simple folded piece of felt, or animal skin, secured by a surcingle. From this was developed a leather pad stuffed with the hair of Equus himself. It was soon noticed that weight pressing directly on a horse's spine—particularly the pro-

minent one of a 'poor doer'—is very liable to cause sores, or galls, so the next brainwave was a pair of pads joined by cross-straps and resting on the dorsal muscles and ribs, leaving the spinal ridge free. Examples of such 'double-pads' were found in the Pazyryk burial sites, and the basic idea is still the principle of the modern saddle. The saddle proper, with arched wooden tree, is said to have been evolved by the Sarmatians, warlike eastern neighbours of the Scythians. These people were probably the world's earliest lancers; unlike the other Asiatic warriors they relied chiefly on the spear when mounted, rather than the bow, and there is evidence that it was used in true shock-action style and not hurled like a javelin, as a bareback rider would have to do if he were not to be unhorsed by the impact.

The stirrup, a simple little device, seems an obvious—and, to some, essential —aid to security in the saddle; yet, oddly enough, it was the last piece of basic riding tack to be invented. In fact, our ancestors had been horsemen for about 1,500 years before it occurred to them that some sort of firm rest for the feet could not only facilitate mounting and afford greater comfort and less fatigue both to horse and man, but would also provide a more stable mobile weapon platform. Polo players know that it is virtually impossible to deliver a powerful stroke without standing in the stirrups, and it is astonishing that the early swordsmen and mounted archers managed to wield their weapons effectively with no support for the feet. The coming of the stirrup was no less beneficial to the animal itself. At a gallop it is much easier for a horse if his rider leans in his stirrups with weight well forward and off the back. Similarly, on a long march with much trotting, it eases the horse's back (not to mention the rider's seat) if the 'rising trot' is employed instead of the bump-

Charles I as seen by Van Dyck, on a monster which could surely never have been foaled! The enormous neck and diminutive head are typical pieces of flattery, to sitter and mount bump-bump in the saddle, which was often blamed as a source of sore backs. Without stirrups the rising trot is impossible, except for very brief periods.

It has been claimed, with some justification, that the stirrup was the most important technical contribution to the art of equitation, and to mounted warfare, since the bitted bridle. Most historians are agreed that the stirrup was evolved around the fourth century AD by that scourge of the civilised world, the Huns from Central Asia, whose barbaric hordes carried it both eastwards and westwards. Stirrups are depicted in a bas-relief from the tomb of the Chinese Emperor T'ai Tsung (627–49) and the first dated examples in Europe are to be seen on the altar frontals of Sant' Ambrogio in Milan, c 835. By about AD 1000 their use was common throughout the West.

The horseman's maxim 'no foot, no horse' is probably as old as horsemanship itself. A lame cavalry horse may often be worse than no horse at all, especially on active service, for he becomes a liability; he cannot take his place in the ranks, but he still needs feeding and ill-afforded attention. The horse's hoof, like the human nail, is a constantly growing horny structure, equipped on the sole with an ingenious shock-absorber in the form of the V-shaped, elastic frog. (The Greeks had a better word for it—'swallow', from its likeness to that bird's forked tail). In the horse's original natural habitat of desert and steppe the hoof needed no artificial protection, since the rate of growth was sufficient to replace normal wear, even when the horse was burdened. Thus the early horsemen of the Middle East and Central Asia always rode unshod—as do some of their successors today. Xenophon, in his account of the retreat of The Ten Thousand, mentions that some Armenian tribesmen showed his men how to 'tie little bags round the feet

of the horses' to enable them to struggle through the snow-clad mountains. But these, of course, cannot be claimed as horseshoes. Despite some lessons thrust upon them in campaigning—Alexander's cavalry force, for instance, was once out of action owing to over-worn hooves— the Greeks remained ignorant of shoeing, and all Xenophon had to say about care of the feet was that they could be 'strengthened' by standing the animal on cartloads of large round stones—a practice which might certainly promote a healthy growth of the frog.

The hipposandals used by the Romans were not true horseshoes; these were iron-soled boots secured by leather thongs. At first glance, such equine footwear might seem to have advantages over the conventional shoe; they need no skill to apply and can be replaced in a matter of minutes. As the Romans must have discovered, however, there were serious drawbacks: numerous sizes were necessary to fit individual horses; the sandals had to be removed frequently to relieve pressure on the foot; stones and gravel were liable to get trapped in them; they wore out just as quickly as normal shoes, and the method of fixing was insecure. Oddly enough, experiments were being made with modern hipposandals at the French cavalry school of Saumur as recently as 1939.

When and by whom the horseshoe proper was invented has not yet been established. Hot shoeing has long been taken for granted, even by the horse himself, but those who witnessed the first experiments must have been astounded to behold a red-hot iron plate being applied to the sole of the animal's foot, amid clouds of smoke, and then, when beaten to shape and cool, affixed by the seemingly hazardous method of hammering nails into the hoof. The Romans are sometimes credited with this remarkable invention, and certainly when they criss-crossed Europe with the first metalled road system any unshod cavalry must have had trouble with the hammer, hammer, hammer of hooves on those hard high roads.

The earliest iron horseshoes of conventional form date from about AD 100. In Britain, some were discovered in a burial site at Colchester and are said to be of Roman origin. For some 1,800 years horseshoeing has been regarded as a necessary evil, demanding considerable skill and not a little expense. A horse in hard work will wear out a new set of shoes within one month, or will at least need a 'remove', so one can imagine the time and cost involved in keeping a regiment of, say, 700 horses properly shod and fit for service. Today, with all the astonishing achievements in science and technology no more effective means of protecting a horse's hoof has been devised than the crude, age-old method of nailing on a piece of non-durable metal. Attempts to introduce plastic materials and do-it-yourself kits have proved unsuccessful.

Since in battle the horse presented a much more vulnerable target than his rider—and if one could not kill the man one tried to kill his mount—it was natural that some thought should be given to protecting him as well as the soldier. Horse armour is often thought to have been a development of the Middle Ages, but its use goes back to the earliest days of the horse in warfare. Before the introduction of chain mail, a simple cloth of quilted material, or sometimes leather, covered the animal's back, flanks and quarters; examples can be seen in artwork of Assyrian and Egyptian times. The Sarmatians are said to have used a form of scale armour made from slices of horses' hooves sewn to leather coverings—surely the only example of the horse's natural products being used to protect him.

Parade or ceremonial armour of the fifteenth century

Plate armour was worn by both Greek and Roman horse soldiers, and Xenophon cogently advises that 'as the rider himself is in extreme danger if anything happens to his horse, the animal also should be armed with a frontlet, breastplate, and thigh-pieces'. However, there is nothing in contemporary art or literature to indicate that such horse armour was ever employed by the Greeks; nothing more than a saddle-cloth is shown.

The ultimate in horse armour was reached in medieval times when the head, neck, fore and hind quarters of the 'great horse' were completely covered with jointed plates weighing some 80lb.

'After God... the Horses'

An old Spanish proverb runs: *Más vale caballo que caudal*—a horse is worth more than riches. Certainly, Spain owes much to the horse; in the days of the Romans and the Normans the native breeds of the Iberian Peninsula were already valued for their performance in war, and in the golden age of the great Spanish empire the Andalusian was famed throughout Europe as a charger for kings and princes. It was the Andalusian that laid the foundation of the proud Lipizzaner stallions of the Spanish Riding School in Vienna and more significantly, it was the Spanish war horses of the conquistadores that helped to change the course of history in the New World.

For more than 700 years before Christopher Columbus set off in search of the Indies, Spain had been occupied by the Arabs; and it was in the southern portion, Al Andaluz, that the Arab-Spanish horse was first bred. There has been much dispute about its true origin. Arabian enthusiasts believe that the Andalusian horses were descended from the offspring of the pure-bred desert stock which the Muslim invaders brought with them to Spain and crossed with the indigenous animals; but the cold facts of history seem to point otherwise. When the Arab general Tariq landed at Gibraltar (*Jebel-al-Tariq*) in 711 he had with him 12,000 cavalrymen—of which a mere twelve (probably the senior officers) were native Arabs from Arabia; the remainder were Berbers, Zenetes and other races from North Africa. It was the same with the subsequent waves: nearly all were what are loosely termed Moors, who no doubt obeyed Arab commanders. Thus, it has been pointed out, notably by Denhardt in his scholarly work *The Horse of the Americas*, that it is extremely unlikely that thousands of horses would have been marched the vast distance from Arabia when there were plenty available just

Francis I of France (by Clonet). He was reputed to be a fine horseman, and we are told that hunting was 'his ruling passion'

opposite the Spanish shores. The truth seems to be that while *some* pure-bred Arab horses were employed to found the celebrated Andalusian breed, the vast majority were Barbs from North Africa.

However, a stronger infusion of pure Arab blood no doubt resulted after 1476 when the Carthusian monastery of Jerez de la Frontera—and others in Andalusia —forbade the use of coarse, heavy stallions from Europe and insisted on nothing but Arabs and Barbs—in those days the serving of God was not considered incompatible with the production of such war *matériel* as troop horses. Some chauvinistic Spanish authorities indignantly deny the influence of *any* foreign blood Arab or Barb, and maintain that the Andalusian is, and always has been, of exclusively Iberian stock.

By the sixteenth century the Spanish horse had become the model for all European painters and sculptors, and few important personages—such as Velasquez's kings and dukes, for instance— would have their equestrian portraits painted unless shown on a proud, cavorting Andalusian. Certainly this breed seems to have made an ideal war horse; standing 15 hands or so, he was big for the time, without coarseness, and up to plenty of weight. Arab blood or no, he exhibited the Arab's hardiness and, above all, the *brio escondido*—hidden mettle— being gentle and kind to handle, but full of latent spirit.

One Spanish war horse which earned a place in history was Babieca. Through some twenty years of campaigning, he was the charger of El Cid, the knightly champion who saved his country from the foreign yoke, and whose heroic deeds are celebrated in the great epic, *Poema del Cid* of the twelfth century. El Cid was born Rodrigo (or Ruy) Diaz in the Castillian village of Vivar near Burgos, about 1040; he rose to distinction as a brave but ruthless freelance soldier, fighting now for his countrymen, now for some Moorish prince—whichever suited him best. He died worn out with sickness and wounds in 1099, and what are claimed to be his remains now lie in Burgos Cathedral. The Arabs dubbed him *Al Sid* (the Lord), and in addition to the Spanish form, El Cid, he is often known in literature as *El Campeador*, The Warrior.

When a lad 'of tender years', he had begged a colt of his godfather, a portly priest known to the family as Peyre Pringos—'Fat Pete'. Together they went to a paddock where a number of mares were grazing with foals at foot; ordering the animals to be rounded up and driven past them, the indulgent Pete bade his godson choose whichever he fancied. The boy stood silent while several nice-looking youngsters frolicked by. Then came a mare with an ugly, scraggy colt at her side. 'This is the one for me!' cried Rodrigo. Dismayed at the lad's ignorance of horseflesh, his godfather exclaimed, '*Babieca!* (stupid) thou has made a foolish choice!' But the young Cid was unabashed: 'This will make a fine horse, and Babieca shall be his name.' As with Alexander, it is only to be expected that a future hero should know better than his elders. Babieca has been depicted as a typical Andalusian, which is understandable, but without evidence; and is often described as white, or grey—the usual distinctive colour for a distinguished personage.

The Cid's first military exploit astride Babieca was the defeat of 'the five Moorish kings', when the horse was not more than three or four years old and his master not yet twenty. In the ancient chronicles of the Cid saga (both Spanish and Moorish) there are references to Babieca as 'a steed without equal', and after the capture of Valencia in 1094 he had become 'famous throughout all Spain'. When King Alfonso of Leon and Castille was invited to

El Cid on Babieca, from *Crónica particular del Cid* (1512). Conventionally, the hero is portrayed in anachronistic mediaeval plate armour, while Babieca, who seems somewhat undersize, is surely stylised

adjudicate at a tournament held to select suitable bridegrooms for El Cid's daughters, Babieca earned royal praise. The king commanded the Cid to put the animal through his paces, 'for I have heard so much about him'. Having given a display of horsemanship which astonished monarch and multitude, the Cid then made the conventional gesture of offering Babieca to his patron. 'God forbid that I should take him!' exclaimed Alfonso, 'A horse like Babieca deserves no other rider than you, my Cid, so that both together you may drive the Moors from the field and go in their pursuit. May God hide his favour from any who would take Babieca from you; for you and this horse have brought us great honour.'

Babieca's final service to the Cid was a macabre one; there can be few chargers who have carried their masters to a posthumous victory. When the great Campeador died in Valencia, the Moors were again besieging the city, and the report of his death spread as much despondency among the besieged as it did elation among the besiegers. This had been foreseen by the Cid, and now his last grotesque orders were carried out. His embalmed body was strapped on Babieca's saddle and secured upright by a contraption of poles and ropes; a shield was hung round the corpse's neck, and a sword propped aloft in the lifeless hand. His beard had been carefully trimmed, and under the helmet the cadaver's features glowed with an 'unearthly luminence'. Thus mounted, El Cid rode Babieca to victory in death as he had done in life. At midnight the Moorish camp was astonished to behold a ghostly host of horsemen, all clad in white and bearing white banners, riding silently out of the gates of the city. In their midst was the tall figure of a knight, gleaming sword upraised, bearded visage eerily alight; *Al Sid* had returned from the dead. Terror-stricken, they fled, to be pursued and slain by the Cid's knights.

After the burial of the Cid's body at the monastery of San Pedro de Cardeña, near Burgos (the remains were removed to Burgos later), Babieca was given honourable retirement nearby. Says the *Chronicle of the Cid*:

And from the day in which the dead body of the Cid was taken off his back, never man was suffered to bestride the horse … and Gil Diaz thought it fitting that the race of the good horse should be continued, and he bought two mares for him, the goodliest that could be found, and when they were in foal he saw that they were well taken care of, and they brought forth the one a male and the other a female, and from these the race of the good horse was kept up in Castille, so that there were afterwards many good and precious horses of his race …

The chronicle goes on to say that Babieca survived his master by two-and-a-half years, and died at the remarkable age of forty. If this is so, he must have been an unusually virile old stallion to have successfully covered those two mares at around thirty-eight years of age.

Babieca was buried outside the gates of the monastery and two elms were planted to shade his grave. In 1948, when the Duke of Alva interested himself in the discovery of the horse's remains, the supposed site was excavated, but nothing was found. The monastery had been considerably enlarged since Babieca's day, and it was concluded that the bones, if extant, lie under the more modern buildings. However, the Duke caused a monument to be erected on the site; while Alexander's Bucephalus had been honoured with a city in his memory, Babieca had to wait more than 1,800 years for a more modest memorial.

'Horses are the most necessary things in the New Country because they frighten the enemy most, and after God, to them belongs the victory,' wrote Pedro de Castañeda de Nagera in his contemporary chronicle of the conquest of the New World, and the sentiment is echoed repeatedly by the conquistadores themselves.

When, in October 1492, Christopher Columbus discovered America by setting foot on San Salvador Island in the Bahamas, he had no cavalry with him—at least, there is no record. But on his second voyage in September 1493 he carried a modest complement of lancers, with their mounts. Among the Archives of the Indies in Madrid is preserved the royal edict of 23 May 1493 from Ferdinand and Isabella, authorising ships and *matériel* for the expedition:

We command that a certain fleet be prepared to send to the islands and mainland which have newly been discovered ... and to prepare the vessels for the Admiral Don Christopher Columbus ... and among those we command to go in the vessels there shall be sent twenty lancers with horses ... and five of these shall take two horses each, and the two horses which they take shall be mares.

This is the first intimation of the appearance of the horse in the New World since prehistoric times. Deliberate provision was made for breeding, by the inclusion of ten mares with the fifteen stallions, and no doubt those selected were good specimens of the fine Andalusian breed—but they did not reach their destination. In January 1494 Columbus wrote to his royal patrons complaining that his crafty cavalrymen had sold the valuable bloodstock before embarking and substituted 'common nags'.

Nevertheless, horses continued to be 'the most necessary things', as is evident from the frequent requests, not only for remounts, but also for brood mares, to be sent from Spain, most of them to be '*de distinguida casta*'—of distinguished breeding. The first part of the New World to be colonised was the island of Hispaniola (Haiti), where by 1500 a stud farm with at least sixty brood mares had been established. The island of Cuba, conquered by Diego Velasquez in 1515, became an important base for the subsequent expeditions to the mainland.

It was during the occupation that a Spanish horse—a single one—first showed his, or rather her, potentialities as a war weapon. One of Velasquez's lieutenants, a *hidalgo* called de Narvaez, was despatched with a platoon of thirty bowmen on a deep reconnaissance mission. Only he himself was mounted—on 'a tricky little mare'. One night his small force was surprised by a horde of 7,000 savages, whose intentions seemed distinctly unfriendly. One of them threw a stone which bowled Narvaez over, but he immediately leaped to his feet and, clad only in his nightshirt, vaulted on to the little mare and galloped headlong into the crowd. This centaur-like apparition so terrified the natives that they turned tail and did not pause until they had covered 'fifty leagues'. Their terror must have been real indeed, for when Velasquez later came up with his main body he found the whole province 'entirely depopulated with the exception of some very old and sick people'.

Velasquez had under his command another Spanish gentleman of fortune who was soon to out-general him. One of the best-known of all the conquistadores, Hernán Cortés was once reputed to boast to the Emperor Charles V: 'I am the man who has given your Majesty more provinces than your royal ancestors left you cities.'

On 4 March 1519 Cortés sailed from Cuba with a fleet of eleven ships, carrying some 800 soldiers, sailors, negroes, Indian women—and sixteen horses. On 12 March they made a landfall on the Mexican coast, near what later became the town of Tabasco, and the force disembarked the same day. Cortés had with him a chronicler who was not only a diligent war correspondent, but also a devoted horseman. When fifty years afterwards he came to write his monumental history of the conquest, Bernal Díaz del Castillo treated the horses with as much affectionate remembrance and detail as if they had been his own human comrades; as Cunninghame Graham observes: 'One feels that he had ridden, fed, and led to water almost all of them'. Thanks to Díaz there is a complete record of the first horses to be seen on the North American continent:

I wish to put down, from memory, all the horses and mares that we disembarked:

Captain Cortés had a dark chestnut stallion which died when we reached San Juan Ulua.

Pedro de Alvarado and Hernando Lopez de Avila had a very good bright bay mare, which turned out excellent both for tilting and for racing when we got to New Spain [Mexico]. Pedro de Alvarado took his share either by purchase or by force.

Alonzo Hernandez Puertocarrero a grey mare. She was fast, and Cortés bought her (for him) for a gold shoulder knot.

Juan Velasquez de Leon another grey mare, and she was very strong. We called her *La Rabona* [Bobtail].

Christoval de Olid had a dark brown horse, that was very satisfactory.

Francisco de Morla a dark bay horse which was very fast and had a good mouth.

Francisco de Montego and Alonzo de Avila, a dark chestnut horse; he was no good for war.

Juan de Escalante, a light bay horse with three white stockings. He was not very good.

Diego de Ordas, a grey mare. She was barren and a pacer, but not fast.

Gonzala Domínguez, an excellent horseman, had a dark brown horse, very good, and fast.

Pedro González de Trujillo, a good bay horse, a beautiful colour, and he galloped well.

Moron, a settler of Bayamo, had a pinto with white forefeet, and he had a good mouth.

Baena, from La Trinidad, had a piebald with white forefeet; he proved worthless.

Lares, a fine horseman, had a good horse, bay in colour, but rather light; he was an excellent galloper.

Ortiz the musician [trumpeter?] and Bartolomé Garcia, who had gold mines, had a black horse called *El Arriero* [Drover]. He was one of the best horses that we took aboard the fleet.

Juan Sedeño from the Havana, a

brown mare, and this mare had a foal on board the ship. This Juan Sedeño was the richest soldier in the fleet, for he had a ship, the mare, a negro, and much cassava bread and bacon.

This prototype muster roll of cavalry raises some interesting points. There is a preponderance of stallions—eleven, to five mares—which is to be expected, for it was still the normal practice to ride only entires. It seems odd, however, that a commander setting forth on an important expedition with some 500 infantry should allow himself a mere handful of sixteen mounted troops, especially as he well knew their value. But horseflesh was still a scarce commodity in the Indies, as Díaz explains: 'In those days there were no horses to be got, or negroes either, except at a great price, and that was why we embarked no more, for there were hardly any to be had'. Some of the soldiers were expected to share one horse, and two of the men could not even ride! And it was surely hazardous to embark a heavily in-foal mare for a sea voyage of unknown duration in a tiny over-crowded vessel. Since she gave birth during that ten-day trip, she must have been uncomfortably large when she embarked, and it is surprising that she survived the ordeal, slung and shackled in the cramped 'tween deck. Unfortunately, Díaz does not say what became of the foal.

Soon after establishing a beachhead, Cortés was involved in a hot skirmish with the 'Indians', who outnumbered his little force by nearly three hundred to one, but the terrifying spectacle of those fantastic creatures from another world, half beast, half man, proved too much for the enemy's nerves, and they fled to the safety of the jungle. The horsemen, as Díaz quaintly records, 'had the opportunity to lance the Indians at their pleasure, a thing most expedient at the time'.

The astute Cortés later arranged a demonstration for the benefit of some friendly Indians. He caused one of the mares who happened to be conveniently in season to be tethered behind his headquarters. When the concourse of natives had been summoned near, the black stallion, who was *muy rijoso* (very lustful), was led forward. Scenting the interesting female, he performed as stallions do in such circumstances: 'He began to trample the ground, roll his eyes and neigh loudly, wild with excitement'. The Indians imagined he was venting his wrath at them, and were petrified lest he should be set upon them. The mare was secretly led away and Cortés, patting and calming the stallion, explained that he had commanded him to do them no harm, since they were friendly.

In his imperial palace in the old city of Mexico, the mighty Montezuma shortly received a report that must have caused him some qualms. Bearded white warriors had come out of the sea, whereon they moved in floating fortified islands; they had weapons that belched flame and smoke, and killed at a great distance; and worse, they had brought strange, fierce monsters like stags without antlers:

The stags came forward, carrying soldiers on their backs . . . These stags snort and bellow. They sweat very much, and the sweat pours from their bodies in streams. The foam from their muzzles drips onto the ground. It spills out in fat drops like the sap of soapplants. They make a loud noise when they run; they make a great din, as if stones were raining on the earth. The ground is pitted and scarred where they set down their hooves: it opens whenever their hooves touch it.

The Aztec emperor was further informed that the fearsome beasts had to be bridled to prevent them from savaging humans, and that they commonly munched the iron bars put in their mouths.

It took Cortés just over two years of unremitting marching and fighting, through jungle, swamp and savannah, to reach the city of Mexico, which surrendered after an heroic defence in August 1521. During this campaign he had received reinforcements of both men and horses, the latter being 'our chiefest need'. The records of the conquest abound in references to the horses. Cortés himself wrote five lengthy reports, or *Relaciones* (now usually known as The Letters of Cortés), to his Emperor, Charles V, in which he related in detail the ebb and flow of their progress.

Men and horses endured days without water, and often when a foetid pool was encountered it proved so foul and stinking that even the thirst-crazed animals refused to touch it. Heat and humidity took their toll—'the grease inside them melted'. In action, Cortés' mini-troops of cavalry were always to the fore, gallantly charging overwhelming numbers, and the battle casualties mounted. Most, both human and equine, were caused by the deadly showers of arrows from bows so powerful that the shafts would pierce a horse's body from flank to flank.

As the campaign wore on, the Aztec warriors became bolder, realising that the strange beasts were as mortal as their riders. In one encounter a daring Aztec wielding a terrible axe decapitated one of the horses at a single stroke. After a mare was lost, Díaz penned a laconic obituary: 'The Indians ate her'. Always in his letters to the Emperor, Cortés bemoans the loss of a horse as though it were one of his most trusty officers. 'They killed a horse also, and God alone knows how great was its value to us, and what pain we suffered at its death: because,

The entry of Cortés into Mexico

after God, our only security was the horses.' However, since they were practically starving at the time, they consoled themselves by devouring the animal's flesh, 'without leaving even the skin'.

The sense of comradeship felt by a horse soldier for his mount has long been traditional, and it is quite clear that Cortés and his men were genuinely grieved at the suffering of their faithful partners. After the fierce, ninety-day siege of Mexico City, Cortés sent off his Third Letter to Charles V, recounting his victory; in the middle of this involved military and political report comes a little aside that is as revealing as it is sincere in its sentiment:

. . . We suffered no loss that day except

that, during the ambush, some of the horsemen collided with each other, and one was thrown from his mare, which galloped directly towards the enemy. They wounded her severely with arrows, and she seeing the ill-treatment she got, returned to us, and that night she died. Although we grieved exceedingly at it, for the horses and mares gave life to us, our grief was less than had she died in the hands of the enemy, as we feared would be the case.

In the days before qualified veterinary officers appeared in the field, treatment of wounded animals was left largely to nature, or to primitive expedience. Díaz gravely tells us that after a skirmish they cauterized their own and their horses' wounds with hot grease 'taken from a fat Indian'.

After the crowning victory of Mexico City, Cortés led his army south to what is now Honduras—a marathon march of nearly 1,000 miles through some of the most difficult terrain in Central America. His force amounted to no more than 300 Spaniards, including about 120 cavalry, and some 2,000 Mexican allies. Hopelessly outnumbered by the Indians, as always, they again relied on the terror inspired by the horses, which had not before been seen in these parts. On one occasion some horses captured an enemy position unaided by their riders; having broken loose, they galloped into the settlement where they caused such alarm and dismay that the whole population took to their heels and abandoned the position. On this march the chief enemy was not the Indians, but the terrain, which varied from low-lying swamp, jungle and wide rivers to 6,000ft mountains, with consequent extremes of temperature. When Cortés eventually reached the little seaport which today bears his name, Puerto Cortés, casualties had

decimated his force. Only forty of his countrymen were still effective; of the 2,000 Mexicans a mere fifty had survived, and sixty-eight horses had succumbed to wounds or exhaustion. Most of those that remained were so poor that they could not be ridden. In his final report to King Charles he added: 'The last horse that I had uninjured was disabled by a fall, and at the time of writing is still unserviceable.'

Cortés originally landed on the shores of Mexico with a chestnut stallion as his personal charger, which 'died when we reached San Juan Ulúa'. It was perhaps understandable that the C-in-C should then appropriate that fine black horse belonging to Ortiz the musician and his gold-miner friend, which Díaz described as one of the best to be embàrked in the fleet; 'Drover' was apparently considered a somewhat undignified name for the animal's elevated status, for Cortés subsequently refers to him as *'mi Morzillo'* (my Black). He must have been an admirable charger, with remarkable stamina; after disembarking at Tabasco in 1509, he endured the campaign of 500-odd miles of marching and fighting which culminated with the capture of Mexico City. He was several times wounded; once receiving an arrow in the mouth. Then he carried his master on the marathon march to Honduras. In all, he must have covered more than 1,500 miles, much of it over some of the worst riding country in the world. But he did not see the goal of the Honduras coast. When within about a hundred miles, Cortés halted for a day at the lake-island city of Tayasal, inhabited by the friendly Maya tribe of Peten Itzas (from whom the lake takes its present name), and here Morzillo's campaigning ended. Cortés wrote to his Emperor: 'My Black got a splinter in his foot and was unable to go on; the chief promised to cure it, but I do not know what he will do with him.' Indeed he never knew, for that was the last he and his men saw of the faithful charger.

Nearly two hundred years elapsed before the next Europeans set foot in Tayasal—a band of Franciscan missionaries intent on converting the idolatrous Maya tribes. They were courteously received and conducted to a vast temple capable of holding a thousand worshippers. In the centre of the temple they were astonished to behold a gigantic stone figure of a horse seated dog-like on its haunches, with eyes, nostrils and open mouth painted a startling scarlet, and at its feet a vivid profusion of tropical flowers and fruit. This, said their guide with due reverence, was Tziminchak, god of thunder and lightning, and the tribe's most potent deity. Many years ago, he went on, some fair-skinned men like themselves had appeared from the lake, mounted on thundering god-beasts such as this. As a token of friendship, one of the beasts was left behind with the chief, who installed it in the temple and caused it to be worshipped, with offerings of chicken, flowers and fruits of the jungle. But despite all this care and attention the beast soon died, and in its place was erected the statue. This was later destroyed by the Christian missionaries, shocked at such ignorant idolatry.

Morzillo can claim to be the only war horse in recorded history to achieve deification. And, according to Denhardt, the native canoe-folk of the town of Remediro, which now occupies the site of Tayasal, will tell you that 'on clear, moonlit nights you may see Tziminchak deep in the waters of the lake, tolerantly receiving the worship of the Itzas while he awaits Cortés' return'.

The exploits of Cortés tend to over-shadow those of other great conquerors and colonists, such as Pizarro and de Soto, who added the vast territories of the South American Incas to the Spanish Empire. All of them paid handsome tribute to the long-suffering horses that never failed to over-awe their enemies and enabled the Spaniards to snatch victories from overwhelming odds. In one fierce action de Soto lost eighty of his best men and forty-five horses, the latter being 'no less mourned and wept for than the men, for in them was the greatest strength of the army'. An even greater tragedy befell when, on the abortive expedition to Florida in 1541, a surprise attack was made on de Soto's camp and eighty of his horses were either shot with flaming arrows or burned to death in their blazing thatched horse-lines: 'Our greatest anguish was not the loss of many brave Christians, but the memory of those demented horses in their suffering, whom we were powerless to help.'

63

Birth of the Cavalry Spirit

With the possible exception of the Arabian, the most widely distributed and highly regarded breed of modern saddle horse is the Thoroughbred—formerly known as the English Thoroughbred, for it was England that nurtured the first stock.

As every bloodstock enthusiast is aware, the Thoroughbred traces his ancestry back to three progenitors: the Byerley Turk, the Darley Arabian and the Godolphin Barb, all of which were in fact Arabians, imported to England between 1684 and 1728. Of this holy trinity of bloodstock, only the 'original begetter', the Byerley Turk, saw military service, thereby staking a claim for himself as the only war horse to have founded a world-famous breed.

Although there is no documentary evidence, the Byerley Turk is reputed to have been one of the numerous Arab horses captured from the Turks when they were driven from Vienna by an allied

This painting of the Wellesley Arabian , by Ben Marshall (1767–1835) is typically flattering as regards height. Unless the human models were unusually small, the animal must be at least 15.3 hands, whereas no pure-bred Arab was more than 15 hands

Christian force in 1683. John Evelyn, in his *Diary* for 17 December 1684, describes three very fine Arab stallions exhibited to King Charles II in St James's Park; they had lately arrived from Hamburg, having been 'taken from a Bashaw (Pasha) at the siege of Vienna' and, he adds, 'there were never seen any horses in these parts to be compared to them'. One of these was no doubt the Byerley, though he had not then acquired this name.

Robert Byerley was a wealthy landed gentleman of Middridge Grange, near Heighington in County Durham; in 1685 he raised a troop of cavalry for the newly-formed 9th Horse* with which he served throughout William III's campaign against James II in Ireland. He was wounded at the Battle of the Boyne and retired as Colonel of the Regiment in 1691. While there is no authentic record of how or when Byerley obtained his 'Turk',† he certainly rode him as his charger at the Boyne, where the 9th's losses were heavy, including sixty-four horses killed and fifty-seven wounded. Byerley took his faithful charger with him into retirement and put him at stud, first at Middridge Grange, and then at Goldsborough Hall near York. The General Stud Book shows that he became the great-great-grandsire of the famous Herod, and his line can be traced down to such twentieth-century giants of the Turf as The Tetrarch and Tourbillon. Apparently Byerley never bestowed a name on him, but then neither did the owners of the Darley Arabian and the Godolphin Barb, and it is simply as the Byerley Turk that

he is known. Despite the noun, he was a pure-bred Arab, standing about 15 hands, bay in colour, with no white on him. The well-known painting by John Wootton (1677–1765) is typical of conventional flattery, depicting an ultra-refined, leggy and herring-gutted animal, far more like the stylised TB racehorse than the Arab charger that he was.

The defeat of the Turks in 1683 was brought about chiefly by the great Polish King John III Sobieski—'the Saviour of Vienna'—with his 20,000 light cavalry, and this monarch's charger Palasz (Sabre) is famed in Polish annals. A cross between Andalusian, oriental and native breeds, Palasz was a big weight-carrying grey stallion who bore his master throughout eleven years' hard campaigning against invading Tartars and Cossacks, and led the devastating charge that shattered the Turks at Vienna. A weight-carrier indeed, for the fifty-four-year-old king was 'of stout proportions' and rode at least 16 stone. An earlier Polish equine hero was Tarant, charger of General Stephan Czarniecki who repulsed a Swedish invasion in 1656 and trounced the Russians in 1660. Tarant is described as a dappled grey oriental gelding; selective breeding had long been established in Poland and it was not beneath the dignity of a senior commander to ride a 'cut' animal. Among Tarant's recorded achievements was a 180-mile forced march in thirty-six hours, leading a relief to the beleagured garrison of Danzig. Although each cavalryman had a spare mount, many of the 6,000 horses succumbed to the pace and the sub-zero temperatures of the January weather, but Tarant carried the C-in-C throughout, with no respite. On a bitter December day of 1658 he and his master 'swam the sea' to capture the Swedish-held island of Alsen, off the Danish mainland; even if the 'sea' was a 350-yard narrows, this was no mean feat.

---

* Later the 6th Dragoon Guards (Carabiniers) and now The Royal Scots Dragoon Guards.
† Some writers allege that Byerley himself captured the animal at Vienna, but this is palpably false. No British troops were involved in the siege, and Byerley's 'foreign' service was limited to the Irish campaign.

Not unnaturally, equine warriors celebrated in history are usually the proud chargers of princes and generalissimos, but there are curiously humble exceptions. One of the earliest English examples is Old Drummer, a survivor of the farcical battle of Sheriffmuir in 1715, lost and won alike by both Royalist and Jacobite opponents. Old Drummer was a drum-horse of The King's Own Dragoons (later the 3rd Hussars); he was subsequently acquired by one Edward Raine, a noted bloodstock owner of Snow Hall, Teesdale, and probably would never have been heard of again had he not lived to the remarkable age of forty-five and earned an obituary in *The Gentleman's Magazine* of February 1753:

Newcastle, January 17. Last week dy'd at Snow Hall near Gainford a drum-horse who was in Gen. Carpenter's regiment at the battle of Sheriff Moor in 1715, being then 7 years old, where

The Duke of Marlborough and his staff at the Battle of Blenheim. The horses, as usual, are heavily stylised, with impossibly thick necks and tiny heads

he received a bullet in his neck, which has been extracted since his death.

He was buried at Gainford, and an epitaph, composed by James Raine and Robert Surtees, reveals that he was oddly unsuited to the martial profession: 'He never lik'd the rattling of a drum, And always dreaded the firing of a gun'. Having been relegated as 'a lady's pad', he disgraced himself by depositing the fair one in the mud; and, as a final humiliation, was put to the cart and the plough:

Which he well perform'd, till with old age oppress'd,
In great content enjoy'd some years of rest.
Yesterday he was the oldest horse alive
Today he's dead, and aged 45.

By the eighteenth century, European cavalry had fully recovered from its temporary melancholia, and under such able commanders as Charles XII of Sweden, Marlborough, and Frederick II of Prussia, it reached its zenith as a mobile striking force. This was the age which

This picture of a British light dragoon, *c* 1790, shows the deplorable contemporary fashion of docking—the 'Cadogan dock'

bred the 'cavalry spirit': the moral and physical superiority of the horseman, thundering in massed squadrons knee-to-knee, sword in hand, trumpets shrilling, crashing through formed bodies of infantry by sheer momentum and weight of numbers. Out of twenty-two major battles fought by Frederick the Great, at least fifteen were won largely by his cavalry.

It was Marlborough who divested the British of their 'pistoleer' complex, which had lingered on in spite of Rupert and Cromwell; he insisted on the use of cold steel alone, even though his squadrons which routed the French at Blenheim and Ramillies did so only at a steady, controlled trot. Not for him the impetuous galloping of Charles XII, who once rode two horses to death while drilling a single regiment.

At this period the British troop horse was developing into the type that became accepted as the ideal for succeeding centuries: a weight-carrying half-bred animal, well-coupled, with plenty of bone, and standing about 15 hands. It seems he was usually a cross between stallions of Barb or Arab strain with English mares, and black was the preferred colour. The custom of mounting regiments of Horse, or heavy cavalry, entirely on blacks or dark browns remained until well into the nineteenth century, and is inherited today by Britain's Household Cavalry with their 16-hand Irish-bred blacks. Marlborough evidently believed in the superiority of the English troop horse; in 1704 Mr Secretary Harley wrote to him suggesting the purchase of German remounts for the forthcoming campaign, but the C-in-C curtly declined, 'having always been of the opinion that English horses, as well as English men, are better than what can be had anywhere else'. During the celebrated 250-mile march to the Danube, his ally Prince Eugene (himself a cavalryman) reviewed the British regiments and was

moved to declare: 'My Lord, I never saw better horses than these.' He also added that money, which was not wanting in England, might buy fine horses, but could not 'buy that lively air I see in every one of these troopers' faces'.

One wonders whether the Prince commented on the regulation disfigurements then inflicted on those fine horses. Their tails were docked so short as to leave nothing but a shaving-brush stump, thus depriving them of their anti-fly defences; and, more barbarous, their ears were cropped almost to the skull. Docking was instigated by Marlborough's own Quarter-Master General, Lord Cadogan, who should have known better, since he commanded Cadogan's Horse (5th Dragoon Guards); his name was perpetuated for many generations afterwards by the term 'Cadogan dock'.* There may have been some logical reasoning for the custom as far as the artillery and transport were concerned, for it might prevent tails becoming entangled in traces, but there was nothing to recommend the practice for the cavalry, except that it relieved the troopers of the chores of brushing out and washing long matted tails—and plaiting them for review order. The pernicious cropping of ears arose, it is said, because so many unfortunate horses had their ears slashed by their own riders when zealously practising the regulation 'six cuts' of mounted sword exercise. *Ergo*, the offending appendages must be removed, otherwise an accident in action might be violently resented by the horse, which could also be blinded by its own blood.

In the War of the Spanish Succession—Marlborough's wars—vast numbers of horses took the field. At Blenheim, for

* *The English, as their savage taste prevails,*
Behead their Kings and cut their horses' tails
(Voltaire)

instance, 20,000 allied cavalry were opposed to 18,000 French. And the fighting soldier depended on the horse for the transport of his field guns, ammunition, rations, baggage and all other impedimenta, not to mention the evacuation of himself if wounded. Thus, in the march to the Danube, the allies needed 2,500 horses for the artillery 'train' and 5,000 more for the commissariat wagons. When dealing with battle casualties, military historians seldom mention the horses, who usually suffered more than the human combatants, and even regimental records are often silent. It was generally reckoned that, on average, horse losses were about one-third greater than those of their riders. At Ramillies, for instance, the 3rd and 6th Dragoon Guards lost 'about 100' horses each, to sixty or seventy men. There were other losses besides battle casualties; the sea transport of horses was always hazardous, and when crossing the North Sea to Holland two British regiments lost eighty horses out of 600. All these casualties involved enormous sums for replacements: the Blenheim campaign cost £6,725 for troop horses.

In the history of European warfare Frederick the Great stands pre-eminent as a cavalry commander. His squadrons performed feats which astonished the rest of the Western world, and the Prussian cavalry set a pattern of excellence which was emulated, but never surpassed, almost down to the present century. The secret of Frederick's success lay in fierce discipline, spartan training of individual man and horse, and close co-operation with the horse artillery—a mobile form of supporting fire-power which he himself invented. As he wrote: 'Every horse and every trooper has been finished with the same care that a watchmaker bestows upon each wheel of the mechanism.' When he succeeded his father, Frederick William I, in 1740, the cavalry were 'colossi on

elephants', huge men on fat horses: the one could not stay in the saddle out of a walk, and the other could not gallop. In short, the cavalry 'were not worth the devil coming to fetch it away'. Yet within ten years his squadrons under Seydlitz and von Ziethen were supreme on the battlefield. This transformation was wrought by ruthless, unremitting drill in the field. Every day the king himself exercised the massed regiments, demanding more and more in horsemanship, endurance and discipline. Previously, parade-ground drill and smartness of turn-out had been all that mattered. If the charge was ever practised, it was done at a sober trot, possibly developing into a daring canter for the last 100 yards. Frederick was not satisfied until his men could charge for one mile over rough ground, the last 800 yards at full gallop, rally, and then repeat the performance. Broken limbs were discounted: 'What signifies that,' he once remarked, 'if it should mean the gaining of a victory?' Hohenfriedburg, Kesseldorf, Rossbach and Freiberg are just a few of the victories that were the fruits of Frederick's genius.

When eulogising the achievements of Frederick and his cavalry, historians have often overlooked the personal attention he devoted to horsemastership, as well as horsemanship, and to the provision of suitable remounts. Better than most military monarchs, he knew that a cavalryman is only as good as his horse when it comes to hard campaigning. *The Regulations for the Hussar Regiments* (1743), personally composed and dictated by the king, are full of precepts which would be applauded by a modern bloodstock trainer. The emphasis was on regular exercise and strict control of feeding. In peacetime 'His Majesty considers it of the highest importance for the preservation of the horse that he should be ridden every day. The horses will then always be in wind, will not be stiff in the legs, and not get fat.' Most of the exercise was to be at the trot, but some galloping was demanded: 'this tends more to preserve rather than to injure the horses'. All squadron officers were to attend daily 'stables' parade and ensure that their men carried out thorough grooming, which was as important as exercise for maintaining condition.* They were to see that each horse received his allotted ration of feed and to report any sick animals at once. Like all practical horsemasters, the king would not tolerate fat horses; wars were won with muscle, not fat, and 'the horses must not be fed so as to be over-conditioned; they want marrow in their bones, not belly'. The daily ration (in peacetime) was 8lb of oats and 11lb of hay or 15lb of chopped straw. The oats 'should be dry and not sunburned, or they will disagree with the horses'. And straw was not to be fed if hay was available, since the former 'bloats the horses without giving them any nourishment'. Green forage (ie grass) was to be given whenever possible.

The Prussian cavalry comprised the usual 'heavy' cuirassiers and dragoons and the 'light' hussars. Horses for the heavy corps were to be at least 15.2 hands, but the hussars, whose height was restricted to 5ft 5in, had lighter animals of 14.3 hands. Frederick's father had already founded what was to become the famous stud of Trakehner horses in East Prussia (now part of the USSR); this he handed over to his son in 1739, and it became the chief source of remount supply for the Prussian army. The Trakehner breed, which is still admired, was of mixed blood, based on the native *Schweiken*

animal with crossings of oriental, English, Danish and other breeds.

Frederick himself had a high opinion of what he called 'the ancient race of English horses', and according to Major-General Sir N. M. Smyth, writing in the *Cavalry Journal* in July 1922, he rode a sixteen-year old English half-bred, Tall Grey, at his first battle of Mollwitz, in 1741. This worthy grey is said to have carried the king on a march of 65 miles on the night of the action, and to have lived to the age of thirty-five.

Another English horse which achieved some distinction in the Seven Years War was a charger of that brilliant cavalry commander, the Marquis of Granby, who added a phrase to the English language by galloping bald-headed for the enemy at Warburg. According to an article in *The Gentleman's Magazine* written in 1793, twenty-three years after the marquis's death:

There is now living and in the possession of a Hawker, a horse which in the Seven Years War was the property of the Marquis of Granby when he commanded the forces engaged in the campaign. This horse when he returned from the Continent was 16 years old. As a reward for his services the Marquis turned the horse out into his Park, where he lived for another 16 years. At the end of this term the horse was sold to his present owner who has worked him regularly for the last 14 years and is now the uncommon age of 46.

The above horse is grey interspersed with bloody spots, and is in good condition and eats well.

The resounding successes of Frederick the Great's horsemen owed much to their supporting horse artillery. With the increase in infantry fire-power it was always a fairly sound maxim that cavalry could

* Cf. British Army manual *Animal Management* (HMSO, 1933): 'The objects of grooming are cleanliness, prevention of disease, and improvement of the animal's condition ...'

Horse artillery of Frederick the Great, which became the model for the rest of Europe.

not overcome formed bodies of infantry without some preliminary 'softening up', preferably by artillery. But, until Frederick's day, field guns could hardly be termed mobile, the cumbersome pieces dragged by heavy cart-horses were often incapable of keeping station with the plodding foot-soldier, let alone the cavalry. At the battle of Warburg an eager young captain of the Royal Artillery astounded both sides by urging his hairy-legged teams into a lumbering canter to bring the guns into action with timely effect.

By 1760 Frederick had devised and introduced the first truly mobile form of *Reitende Artillerie*. The light 6-pounder guns were each drawn by six horses, in pairs, the drivers riding postillion-wise on the nearside horses; the gunners were mounted, not on the limbers as was first proposed, but on horses of their own, so as to reduce the weight behind the teams. For the first time the cavalryman could expect fire support when and where he wanted it; it was soon the horse gunner's proud boast that, wherever the cavalry went, the 'galloping gunners' would go too. Frederick's brain-child was copied first by the French, and in 1793 the British corps d'élite, the Royal Horse Artillery, was formed on exactly the same pattern.

The introduction of horse artillery necessitated a new type of horse for military service: a dual-purpose 'ride-and-drive' animal which could pull its weight in the team, drawing about $1\frac{1}{2}$ tons of gun and limber, and keep pace with the cavalry. The RHA remounts had to be between $15.0\frac{1}{2}$ and 15.2 hh, not more than six years old when bought, and bay, brown or chestnut. When the first troop was raised in February 1793, it was mounted exclusively on chestnuts and has ever since been known as 'The Chestnut Troop' ('A' Battery).

Until the last decades of the eighteenth century, little thought was given to the care of horse casualties in the field. There were no veterinary services; one or two illiterate farriers per squadron kept the horses on their legs by ensuring that they were properly shod. While some horsemen undoubtedly grieved at the sufferings of their mounts, many others seem to have been remarkably callous. When his horse was badly hit in the stomach, one of von Ziethen's hussar officers mounted another and went about his business. On a withdrawal the following day, he happened to

pass the stricken animal lying where it had fallen, with its entrails tangled in its legs. His only comment was, 'I was surprised to observe the horse lift its head as we rode by.' Later, during the Peninsular campaign, Lieutenant William Swabey of 'E' Troop RHA was wounded and evacuated to an aid centre, where he was amused to find a brother officer 'actually in tears at the loss of his horse. I laughed at him and told him the state *I* was in, but he still kept prating about the horse'. General de Marbot describes how one of his fellow chasseurs, Captain Labédoyère, was riding a nervous young horse in Spain, when it became frightened at the sound of gunfire and refused to go on. Whereupon the officer leapt off in a rage, drew his sword and promptly hamstrung

the unhappy animal, 'who fell all bleeding on the grass, dragging himself along on his forefeet'.

The horse was often regarded as no more than a mobile weapon platform; moreover, it was not a good thing for a soldier to become sentimental over his mount. His duty was to fight, not to mope and bemoan the loss of a pal—equine or human; that was bad for morale. A badly wounded horse could not readily be evacuated from the battlefield; if only one of his four limbs was broken, it was unlikely he would ever be fit for service again, and the only answer was the bullet.

In the early years of the nineteenth century, European cavalry was organised much in the form it was to retain until within living memory. The smallest tacti-

The Byerley Turk, Colonel Robert Byerley's charger at the Battle of the Boyne, and progenitor of the English Thoroughbred. In this idealised study by Wootton he is scarcely recognisable as a pure-bred Arab of 15 hands

In the field with Napoleon's Polish Lancers, *c* 1810

cal unit was the troop of some thirty men and horses under a captain; four or more troops formed a squadron—a major's command—and a regiment usually comprised four squadrons with a lieutenant-colonel, or sometimes full colonel, as commanding officer. Total strength varied; a British regiment's war establishment seldom exceeded 600 all ranks, with possibly 700 horses, but Napoleon's cuirassiers and *chasseurs à cheval* often numbered 1,000 officers and men. While a trooper was allowed only one mount, an officer was expected to maintain (and pay for) at least three chargers, plus many others for his entourage of servants and baggage. When Lieutenant-Colonel Hussey Vivian took the 7th Hussars to the Peninsular campaign in 1813, he equipped himself with seven horses, four mules and one pony.

Cavalry were still classified as 'heavy' and 'light'. Though, in theory at any rate, the light cavalry of hussars and (in the British service) light dragoons were supposed to be essentially reconnaissance troops, the blurring of operational roles had already begun, and they were expected to charge with the best of their 'heavy' comrades—the cuirassiers and dragoons—even if mounted on lighter horses of 14.3 hands. While carbine and pistols were now part of the cavalryman's personal armoury, the sword was to be cherished as his true weapon almost until his horse was replaced by the motorised vehicle. Body armour had disappeared, except for the breast- and back-plates of the cuirassiers.

Emperor and Duke

The Russian grenadier with redoubled fury made another thrust at me, but, stumbling with the force which he put into it, drove his bayonet into my mare's thigh. Her ferocious instincts being aroused by the pain, she sprang at the Russian and at one mouthful tore off his nose, lips, eyebrows and all the skin off his face, making of him a living death's head, dripping with blood. Then hurling herself with fury among the combatants, kicking and biting, Lisette upset everything that she met in her path. The officer who had made so many attempts to strike me tried to grab her bridle; she seized him by his belly and carrying him off with ease, bore him out of the crush to the foot of the hillock where, having torn out his entrails and mashed his

Seen in Light Dragoon review order finery this well-bred animal is believed to be a charger of Lord Henry Paget's, who as Lord Uxbridge commanded Wellington's cavalry at Waterloo and later became 1st Marquess of Anglesey

body under her feet, left him dead on the snow. Then, taking the road by which we had come, she made her way at full gallop towards the cemetery of Eylau. Thanks to the hussar's saddle in which I was sitting, I kept my seat . . . But this last spurt had exhausted Lisette's strength; she had lost much blood, for one of the veins in her thigh had been severed, and the poor animal collapsed suddenly and fell on one side, rolling me over on the other.

So wrote a young captain of Napoleon's chasseurs, later to become Lieutenant-General Baron de Marbot. His memoirs are typical of the remarkable spate of literary talent that emanated from combatants of all sides during the Napoleonic wars; probably no other campaigns have been so fully documented with personal recollections, recorded in diaries carried in sabretache or pack and scribbled in the field.

Baron de Marbot, who was the model for Conan Doyle's swashbuckling hero 'Brigadier Gerard', served in all Napoleon's campaigns. He had bought his mare, Lisette, in 1805 for a give-away price of 1,000 francs from a wealthy Swiss banker who had paid 5,000 francs for her—only to discover that she had a little trick of disembowelling her grooms, and would furiously attack anyone else of whom she disapproved. Marbot's cunning servant had a trick of his own: arming himself with a sizzling hot roast leg of mutton, he thrust it at the mare as she advanced to the attack—one bite of that scorching flesh was sufficient. Marbot himself tried the same ruse, and after that the two men could do anything with her. 'She even became more tractable to the stable staff whom she saw every day; but woe to the strangers who passed near her!'

Marbot rode her for two long years of campaigning. After the battle of Fried-land, in 1807, the mare, temper subdued by the ardours of active service, was retired on long loan to the Accountant-General, de Launay, and apparently became a model ladies' hack: 'he let his wife ride her and kept her until she died of old age seven or eight years later'.

When Napoleon became First Consul in 1799 he found his mounted arm in a poor state and took immediate steps to improve it. Before the Revolution, France had become the centre of the 'scientific' school of horsemanship, producing in François de la Guérinière one of the world's greatest exponents. His *Ecole de Cavalerie* (1733) had introduced such movements as the 'shoulder in', the counter canter, flying changes and others which are now regarded as *de rigueur* in the dressage horse. In 1771, when the French cavalry school was opened at Saumur, several state studs ensured a supply of good-quality remounts. The holocaust of the Revolution had swept all this away; with the characteristic fanaticism of egalitarians, everything that smacked of the *ancien régime*, good or bad, was ruthlessly destroyed, and horseflesh and horsemanship deteriorated accordingly. As late as 1807 the French dragoons were described as little more than a rabble on 14-hand ponies.

The Saumur school was not revived until 1815, but in 1806 Napoleon created six national studs, thirty stallion centres and three riding schools. Many of the 1,500-odd stallions at stud were rescued from the old establishments, and there was a generous infusion of Arab blood from horses captured in Egypt and Syria. Throughout the wars of the First Empire the French cavalry proved themselves valorous, disciplined and capable of supreme efforts, but in general their horsemastership was poor. Napoleon himself was little concerned about horse wastage: 'I do not wish the horses to be spared if they can catch men'; and his cavalry was not to be employed 'with any miserly desire to keep it intact'. Despite such able leaders as Kellermann and Murat, the French horsemen lacked the hell-for-leather dash of their British opponents, though this characteristic had its drawbacks. Wellington—an infantry-man by upbringing—was constantly re-proving his cavalry officers for 'galloping at everything' with little thought for control or rally. The French cavalry, he sourly remarked, won battles for the emperor; his only got him into scrapes.

Much of this British 'cavalry spirit' stemmed from the hunting field, where the fox had ousted hare and deer as the quarry, resulting in fast runs across country, with all their exhilarating hazards. Not only did foxhunting breed a thrusting, hard-riding cavalryman, un-daunted by any obstacle, but it also saw the evolution of that ideal type of cavalry horse, the hunter. With a large admixture of Thoroughbred blood, he was well able to carry weight throughout a hard day with hounds and to put in lengthy bursts of speed at almost racing pace. Thus Wellington's cavalry always charged at full gallop (even if they sometimes got out of hand); Murat merely demanded that his squadrons should 'walk on the march and trot in the presence of the enemy'.

On service, the heaviest horse wastage was usually caused by privation and poor horsemastership rather than by enemy action. In Napoleon's Russian campaign Murat lost 18,000 out of 43,000 troop horses in two months. Short of forage, they were kept saddled up for sixteen hours a day, the men never bothering to dismount. General Nansouty, command-ing the Cavalry of the Guard, wryly observed: 'The horses of the Cuirassiers, not unfortunately being able to sustain themselves on their patriotism, fell down by the roadside and died.' On the disastrous retreat from Moscow in 1812, no fewer than 30,000 horses perished, nearly all through starvation and cold; out of the 4,000 horses of the Guard Cavalry only 773 survived. The men could at least find sustenance from the dead animals, whose raw flesh they savagely tore and devoured. General Count de Segur gives the gruesome picture of a badly wounded dragoon who sought both warmth and nourishment by packing himself into the ripped-open belly of a dead horse.

Whether the British horses fared any better than the French in the Peninsular Wars from 1808 to 1814 is debatable. Their sufferings were in large measure due to shortage of forage, extremes of temperature, and gruelling work—in short 'the exigencies of the service'. Some contemporary writers held that the English trooper was little better than his French opposite number when it came to animal management in the field. Captain A. C. Mercer, of 'G' Troop, RHA, wrote in his *Journal of the Waterloo Campaign*: 'In the Peninsula the only means of enforcing some attention to their horses amongst our English regiments was to make every man walk and carry his saddle-bags whose horse died or was sick.' On the other hand, Lord Moira (afterwards 1st Marquess of Hastings) noted in his *Private Journal* that the British soldier 'would as soon see his comrade killed as his horse', which had an equal regard for his master. Moira quotes the touching instance of a dead dragoon's mount found grazing close by the corpse after two days, and refusing to leave it.

The loss of horseflesh, from whatever cause, in the Peninsular campaign was shocking. Less than ten months after Wellington had disembarked in Portugal he was complaining that his cavalry had lost many hundreds and the artillery (above 200) for want of suitable forage.

The chief trouble was that the well-bred, oat-fed animals simply could not accustom themselves to Indian corn, rye, chopped straw, and even gorse at times. Barley, said the Duke, was 'the only wholesome food for horses in this country', but barley was in short supply, and even when obtainable it could not be fed to the English horses without some laborious treatment, such as boiling or parching, otherwise severe digestive troubles resulted. Throughout his general orders, Wellington constantly urged attention to feeding practice: 'Great care should be taken when rye is given to the horses that they are not watered two hours before or two hours after they are fed. The same rule should be observed when they are fed with Indian corn or barley.' Always scathing about his mounted arm, Wellington brooked no excuses for lack of condition among the horses, and threatened to dismount one regiment of light dragoons and pack them off in disgrace to England if there was no improvement.

In his *Despatches*, the duke was no less attentive to the quality of remounts to be sent from England, insisting that they should be at least six years old, preferably not under 15 hands for the cavalry and horse artillery, and, oddly enough, that 'mares should be sent in preference to horses, as it has been found that they bear the work better than the horses'. By 'horses' he probably meant geldings, for stallions were no longer generally employed as troop horses. The price of horseflesh in England had evidently increased since the £12 per remount of Marlborough's day, for the army paid 25 guineas for a troop horse (plus £10 for shipment). An officer had to find £60 out of his own pocket for a first charger, but this was chickenfeed to many wealthy cavalry officers, some of whom did not scruple to hazard their own valuable Thoroughbreds which they brought with

them. Lieutenant-Colonel Edward Kerrison of the 7th Hussars rode a very fine TB named Blake, for which he had refused an offer of 500 guineas from the Prince of Wales.

The disastrous retreat of Sir John Moore to Corunna in the bitter December and January of 1808–9 caused some of the worst losses of the whole Peninsular war. Lord Paget's cavalry actions of Sahagun and Benavente against vastly superior numbers had imbued a healthy respect in the enemy, with trifling British casualties, but the dreadful forced march through the snow and ice of the Galician mountains took its toll. Men and horses—and women and children—dropped in their scores at night, their frozen corpses found by the rearguard on the morrow. An advanced patrol of French dragoons espied a British cavalry vedette huddled on his horse by the roadside. On getting no response to their challenge or their carbine shots, they closed on him to find horse and rider lifeless, frozen 'as though a stone statue'. By the time the unhappy Moore had struggled into Corunna his cavalry were almost literally decimated; two months previously Kerrison's hussars had landed there with something more than 700 horses, now they could muster only seventy.

Then befell to the cavalrymen the most harrowing task they could be asked to perform. Some of the evacuation fleet had been misdirected to Vigo instead of Corunna; thus there were insufficient vessels to accommodate all the remnants of the cavalry horses and, rather than allow the French to capture them, orders were given to destroy all that could not be embarked. A horrifying carnage ensued; there was no time for humane considerations—only a mass slaughter, with troopers, unused to pistols, firing into the demented herds. Maimed and mangled horses struggled or lay still on the

Denis Dighton's impression of a skirmish between the British 14th Light Dragoons and French hussars in the Peninsula (c 1813)

quayside and in the narrow streets. Some, panic-stricken, galloped over the edge of the quay and were left to drown; others fled through the streets pursued by sweating men and erratic shots. When ammunition ran short, the troops were ordered to use the sword, and even worse butchery ensued. Said Captain Gordon of the 15th Hussars: 'The town exhibited the appearance of a vast slaughterhouse.' A Rifleman was moved to record: 'Never did I behold such a dreadful spectacle, and I trust that I shall never again witness the like.'

Most of the officers' chargers were spared and embarked, among them Blake, Colonel Kerrison's Thoroughbred, which, though wounded, had carried him throughout the campaign. But the horse did not reach England; the transport was wrecked off the Lizard and went down with all hands. Kerrison, who had sailed separately, lived to fight at Waterloo.

Sir Godfrey Webster's servant could not bring himself to slaughter his master's faithful Thoroughbred; stripping off the saddlery and accoutrements, he led him to the outskirts of the town and sent him galloping off. The animal ran straight into the French lines, where, being admired for his obvious breeding, he was eventually shown to Marshal Soult, who promptly commandeered him. The Marshal had found a valuable prize, for his new charger was the well-known Pedestrian, bred by the Prince of Wales in 1802, and the winner of many plates and matches at Newmarket.

Another war horse of the Peninsular campaign was Bob, a bright bay gelding ridden by Captain Tomkinson of the 16th Light Dragoons. His war service had begun in 1809 with disgrace; on being embarked at Falmouth he kicked himself out of his slings on the main deck and sent the ship's second mate flying overboard. However, he retrieved his good name later when, with Tomkinson severely

wounded and helpless, he scattered the attacking French infantry and brought him safely out of action. In 1813, Bob returned safely to his stables at Dorfold Hall, Cheshire, and went on to carry his master for several seasons with the family pack of harriers.

Captain (later General Sir) Thomas Brotherton of the 14th Light Dragoons had a beautiful Arabian mare, Fatima:

She was bought by my father at the sale of the King's stud, at three years old. She was of the purest Arabian blood and perfect symmetry, 15 hands high, dark brown, a perfect picture, but very conceited . . . She was the admiration of the whole army. She always wore a silken net to protect her from the flies that maddened her when she hadn't it on. She was wounded several times. At Salamanca a shell shattered her stifle, or thigh, and I was nearly advised to shoot her as incurable, but the stud groom of Lord Charles Manners effected a perfect cure, leaving only an immense scar and dent. She was twice wounded by sabre-cuts on the head. The last time was in the *mêlée* on December 13, 1813 when I was taken prisoner, and she actually reared and pawed my antagonist, as if to defend me. She had her head cut open in a dreadful way.*

Both Fatima and Brotherton were captured on that unlucky 13 December in the Basses Pyrénées, and though the captain eventually rejoined his unit the mare did not. She was too valuable to be

* Hamilton, Col H. B. *Historical Record of the 14th (King's) Hussars* (1901).

This picture of Marengo, by an unidentified artist, was probably drawn after the horse had been purchased by Lieutenant-General J. J. W. Angerstein and put to stud at New Barnes, near Ely

Napoleon, on Marengo, withdraws with his staff at Waterloo

released—Brotherton was once offered 300 guineas for her—and was sent to a French government stud. She no doubt mourned the loss of her master as he did her: 'In bivouac when lying down beside me, she would lift up her head to see if I was sleeping, and if she saw I was, she would immediately lie down again, for fear of disturbing me.' She had a very fiery temperament, which may possibly have resulted from her unusual fondness for raw beef-steaks: 'it was difficult to keep the men's rations from her, even if suspended on trees, as they usually were . . .'

In a Despatch of May 1811, Wellington described the Peninsula as 'the grave of horses'. This fact is well illustrated by the losses of the 14th Light Dragoons, who fought throughout the six-year campaign. In 1808 they landed at Lisbon with their establishment of 720 chargers and troop horses, and during the war received more than 1,120 remounts. When they finally marched into their home barracks at Weymouth in 1814 their horse strength was down to 278—the losses thus amounted to 1,564; casualties among the men were 654.

The most celebrated horses of the Napoleonic wars are the personal chargers —Marengo and Copenhagen—of the two opposing commanders.

Napoleon had acquired at least seven Arab horses during his Egyptian and Syrian campaigns of 1798–9, some being subsequently named after famous battles and sieges: Jaffa, Wagram, Austerlitz, Pyramid. But the one which, rightly or wrongly, has always outshone the others in public esteem is Marengo. A pure-bred Arabian, he was a grey stallion, captured at Aboukir in 1798. He stood only 14.1 hands and, if Meissionier and other artists have portrayed him as a much more imposing animal, it was considered almost *lese-majesté* to show a great conqueror mounted on a pony, and Napoleon himself was no more than 5ft 6in. It is often claimed that the emperor rode Marengo throughout all his campaigns and major engagements from the Battle of Marengo (1800) to the final defeat fifteen years later at Waterloo, but this is highly improbable. Besides his six other Arabs, his normal entourage included no fewer than 200 saddle horses, in addition to carriage horses, and no commander would be likely to ride a single horse through fifteen years' active service. Some sceptics even doubt Marengo's claim to a Waterloo medal; there seems to be no firm evidence that he was present, and the grey that Napoleon certainly did ride on that fateful day could well have been one of the other Arabs. As Major-General W. Tweedie says in his definitive work, *The Arabian Horse*: 'In twenty years, nineteen chargers were killed under Napoleon in sixty general engagements; and the chronicler is unborn who can unfold the histories of his Marengo, Marie, Austerlitz, Ali and Jaffa, all of whom were either grey or white in colour. All that can be certainly said on this point is that a white Arab became part of the Napoleonic legend.'

The circumstances of Marengo's capture are not known, but after Waterloo he was acquired by Lord Petre, and was exhibited in London, together with Napoleon's travelling coach-and-six. The coach horses were sold off by auction, and the carriage was later displayed in Madame Tussaud's, until it was unhappily destroyed in the disastrous fire of 1925. Lord Petre subsequently sold Marengo to Lieutenant-General J. J. W. Angerstein, formerly of the Grenadier Guards, who added him to his bloodstock stud at New Barnes,

near Ely. Here the old warrior remained until his death in 1832, siring some offspring which, apparently, failed to distinguish themselves on the Turf. In the Racing Calendar of 1831 there is an entry of a grey colt 'by the Napoleon Arabian' which ran unplaced at the Newmarket Spring Meeting. After Marengo's death, his skeleton was presented to the Royal United Service Institution, in London, and placed on display in the museum until it was acquired by the National Army Museum, London, where it can still be seen. The animal's hooves were made into snuff boxes; one of these was presented by General Angerstein to the Brigade of Guards and is now preserved in the guardroom at St James's Palace.

Like Napoleon, the Duke of Wellington had numerous chargers during his command—he lost twelve during the first three years in the Peninsula—but, inevitably, it is the animal he rode at Waterloo that has achieved fame. Copenhagen was a chestnut TB stallion, 15.1 hands, a good looker, but of somewhat uncertain temperament. Foaled in 1808, he was of aristocratic blood, for his grandsire was the unbeaten Eclipse (bred by another great soldier, the Duke of Cumberland), while his dam, Lady Catherine, was sired by John Bull, winner of the 1792 Derby. Lady Catherine was the charger of Colonel (later Field Marshal) Earl Grosvenor, who took her on the expedition to Copenhagen in August 1807. Here she was found to be in foal and, as befitting a lady of breeding, was promptly evacuated to England. As a sort of private battle honour, her colt was christened after the victorious siege.

Lord Grosvenor had high hopes of the young Copenhagen on the Turf, but he was disappointed; though the horse ran ten races as a three-year-old, he could not emulate his distinguished grandsire. His name was expunged from the General Stud Book when it was discovered that his granddam was not a Thoroughbred at all, but only a hunter mare of dubious pedigree. Grosvenor then sold the animal to General Sir Charles Stewart, Adjutant-General to Wellington in the Peninsula. On being invalided home in 1812, Stewart passed on his young charger to his chief (for 400 guineas); thus at the tender age of four the failed racehorse began a military career and served for the rest of the Peninsular campaign.

A spirited Thoroughbred, Copenhagen is said to have behaved with remarkable composure under fire, and to have had exceptional stamina. Wellington rode him throughout the final Waterloo campaign of 1815. At Quatre Bras, with the brave abandon of contemporary senior commanders, he was observing the enemy from an exposed forward position. Immediately behind him lay a stiff fence and ditch lined by a battalion of the 92nd Highlanders. Suddenly some squadrons of French dragoons appeared and thundered down upon the sombre-coated figure on the chestnut horse. Shouting to the Highlanders to lie down, Wellington put Copenhagen at the obstacle, and in best hunting-field style cleared fence, ditch, soldiery and all, leaving the confounded dragoons to be received by a volley from Brown Bess.

Both Wellington and his charger miraculously survived unscathed on the field of Waterloo, though there was a nasty moment when the roundshot that smashed Lord Uxbridge's leg missed them by a hair's breadth. Copenhagen lived to enjoy honourable retirement at the duke's country seat of Stratfield saye, near Reading, where he occasionally carried his master in the less hazardous pursuit of the fox. In his old age he was a great pet of the family, particularly of the duchess, who wrote 'he trots after me eating bread out of my hand, and wagging his tail like

Copenhagen as depicted by James Ward RA at the Stratfieldsaye estate of the Duke of Wellington in 1824

a little dog'. On his death in 1836, at the age of twenty-eight, Copenhagen was honoured with an obituary in *The Times*:

DEATH OF A FAMOUS WATERLOO HERO

On the 12th of February died at Straithfieldsaye, of old age, Copenhagen, the horse which carried the Duke of Wellington so nobly on the field of Waterloo . . . He lost an eye some years before his death, and has not been used by the noble owner for any purpose during the last ten years. By the orders of his Grace a salute was fired over his grave, and thus he was buried as he had lived, with military honours. This horse has long been an attraction to strangers, who were accustomed to feed him over the rails with bread, and the Duke himself preserved a special regard for him, which cannot be wondered at, upon considering that he bore him for 16 hours safe through the grandest battle that has occurred in the history of the world. The late amiable Duchess was likewise particularly attached to him, and wore a bracelet made from his hair.

The Iron Duke was seldom given to sentiment, least of all over a horse, but he was moved to add a tribute of his own: 'There may have been faster horses, no doubt many handsomer; but for bottom and endurance I never saw his fellow.' Later on, when it occurred to the authorities of the Royal United Service Institution that it would be fitting for Copenhagen's skeleton to be displayed alongside that of Marengo in their museum, His Grace curtly refused them permission to disturb the honoured bones, which have thus lain in peace to this day.

Greatly to his displeasure, the duke noticed that one hoof had been severed before Copenhagen's burial. Years later that very mild old gentleman, the 2nd

Duke, was much surprised when an aged retainer was ushered into his presence bearing an object wrapped in a copy of *The Times*. It was the missing hoof, and sheepishly the servant confessed to being the culprit; he could never bring himself to face the wrath of the Iron Duke himself.

In the same year that Copenhagen died, there passed away another equine warrior of the Hundred Days. On 20 June 1836 the last surviving Waterloo troop horse of the 2nd Life Guards was put down in Knightsbridge Barracks, at the age of twenty-seven, and buried in Hyde Park. On each anniversary of the battle, Waterloo Jack had been decked with laurels and paraded at the head of the Regiment.

That 'near run thing' of 18 June 1815 was the last major engagement in European history when massed cavalry was used as the principal assault force; Wellington commanded some 13,000 horsemen, Napoleon nearly 16,000. Paradoxically, Waterloo saw both triumph and defeat for the charging squadrons. The British heavy brigades of some 2,000 sabres galloped through a complete infantry corps, two field batteries and a cavalry brigade, rendering them virtually *hors de combat* for the rest of the day. Ney's 5,000 cuirassiers and dragoons, smashing against the stolid squares of allied infantry and canister-spewing guns 'so that the very earth shook', had no more effect than waves bursting against rock; shattered, they left behind men and horses piled upon each other like breastworks under the muzzles of musket and gun.

One of the most vivid personal accounts of the battle is the *Journàl* of Captain A. C. Mercer whose 'G' Troop, Royal Horse Artillery, was virtually wrecked by counter-battery fire. Mercer was justly

'Ces terribles chevaux grises . . .' Royal Scots Greys hack their way through Napoleon's Cuirassiers at Waterloo—as imagined by R. Caton Woodville

R.Caton Woodville.

proud of his 200 sleek, corn-fed horses which, three weeks earlier, had been admired by Blücher during one of the grand reviews: '*Mein Gott,* there is not one horse in this Battery which is not good for a Field-Marshal.' Within less than nine hours at Waterloo, 140 of them lay mangled—dead, dying or hopelessly wounded. Mercer's diary emphasises the stark realities of war in the 'glorious' days of boot-and-saddle. At the height of the battle he noticed some of his drivers un-harness a horse from one of the teams in rear of the gun position and shoo it away. Moments later he was surprised to see the same animal crowding in against the lead-horses of another team, as if seeking their company. He looked down, and was sickened. The animal had only half a bloody head; a cannon shot had completely carried away the lower part immediately below the eyes. 'Still he lived, and seemed conscious of all around, whilst his full, clear eyes seemed to implore us not to chase him from his companions.' Mercer ordered a farrier to end his suffering, which he did by thrusting a sword into the animal's heart—'even *he* expressed feeling on this occasion'.

In those brave times when it was considered undignified to take cover from enemy fire, a battery's gun-teams and led horses formed up directly in rear of the guns, and all officers remained mounted. In a lull between cavalry attacks, Mercer was conversing with one of his troop subalterns, whose jaded horse was standing at an angle to his own and dozily resting its muzzle on his thigh. The officer, no

Escorted by cavalry and horse artillery, Wellington's force crosses the Bidassoa River into French territory, October 1813. The artist, J. P. Beadle, has allowed himself some conventional licence in the immaculate condition and turn-out of both horses and men. But he is remarkably accurate with uniforms and saddlery, and in his depiction of a trumpeter on a grey less jaded, was leaning over on the animal's head when a roundshot smashed it to pulp and the corpse sank to the ground. Both officers were unscathed, though the subaltern 'looked pale'.

Mercer's fine troop was so badly mauled that it could not take part in the final pursuit, and the remnants suffered a horrifying night among the carnage on the field:

Horses, too, there were to claim our pity—mild, patient, enduring. Some lay on the ground with their entrails hanging out, and yet they lived . . . One poor animal excited painful interest—he had lost, I believe, both his hind legs; and there he sat the long night through on his tail, looking about as if in expectation of coming aid, sending forth from time to time long and protracted melancholy neighing.

Though Mercer admits he should have given it the *coup de grâce*, he had, he writes, seen so much blood shed that day he could not bring himself to shed more. When the remainder of the troop pulled out in the morning, the sufferer still squatted there 'neighing after us, as if reproaching our desertion of him in the hour of need'.

Sergeant Ewart of the Royal Scots Greys captures a French 'Eagle' at Waterloo. He was later commissioned for his valour on that day

Theirs Not to Reason Why

For almost forty years after Waterloo the European powers were at peace, except for minor bickerings, and any lessons learned during the previous twenty-two years' campaigning were ignored or forgotten. 'Soldiering is something we do between wars,' as one writer later put it, and armies reverted to the customary military pastimes of clockwork parade-ground drill and stylised review evolutions.

This period saw certain significant developments which aroused more head-shakings about the value of the horseman on the battlefield. The flintlock musket gave way to the percussion-lock rifle, accurate up to 800 yards and far more reliable than its predecessor; a French

'The Remnants of an Army'. Dr Brydon and his wounded horse struggle into Jalalabad after the retreat from Kabul, 1842 (see p 93)

officer, Captain Minié, produced a high-velocity conoidal bullet which could be used with the muzzle-loading rifles, and other minds were busy with murderous multi-barrelled weapons which eventually in the Mitrailleuse and the Gatling gun, gave the infantry unprecedented fire-power. The deadly bullet-spewing field-gun projectile invented, before Waterloo, by a young English artilleryman, Henry Shrapnel, was no longer used exclusively by the British gunner.

But, for the time being, cavalry remained the most mobile and flexible form of striking force. During the reign of Queen Victoria the British Army was involved in more than eighty major and minor campaigns, most of them in the East; in all of them the horse was as essential as the soldier himself.

The vast continent of India, with its varied terrain, offered a training ground unequalled in England, while the troops seldom stagnated in barracks; there was almost constant active service, against foes more ruthless and unconventional than any they had met in Europe. For the cavalry, service in India meant experience with unfamiliar breeds of horses; it was not practicable, or economic, for a regiment's horses to make a voyage of 5,000-odd miles, so they were left at home and others were taken over on arrival. In the early days of the Honourable East India Company, these mounts were chiefly country-bred types, such as the excellent Kathiawari, a small 14 to 14.2 hh animal, fast and hardy. There were seldom more than half a dozen British—or Queen's—cavalry regiments in India at any one time, but the Company had begun raising Indian regiments, with British officers, in the 1770s; these, together with the Company's infantry regiments, were the nucleus of the Indian Army, which was taken over by the Crown after the Mutiny.

At first all cavalry had to find their own horses, which were purchased in the open market or, when opportunity offered, captured from the enemy; after the storming of Seringapatam in 1799, Lord Cornwallis found himself richer by 3,000 troop horses. The East India Company established stud farms in 1794, and by 1810 a remount department had been formed to take over purchasing and supply.

For the next half century or so there was much debate about the best type of mount for the cavalry in India. At home, British regiments swore by their big, well-bred hunter breed with Thoroughbred blood, and maintained that no animal under 15 hands could carry the 20-odd stone of a trooper in full marching order. In India, the doughty little Arab soon changed their minds; by the early 1800s it was being imported in large numbers from the Persian Gulf and for many years was acknowledged as superior to all other breeds for endurance. After the disastrous campaign in Afghanistan of 1839–42, in which horse wastage was appalling, General Sir James Outram reported 'that the Arab and Persian horses stand their work and privations infinitely better than stud and country-breds. The latter, although younger and in far better condition at starting, have invariably been the first to give in, while they seldom rallied afterwards. A few Cape horses lately imported to the Bombay Army have also proved themselves superior to our stud-breds'.

In 1853, Captain Louis Nolan (of Light Brigade fame) also praised Arab and Persian remounts in his *Cavalry; its History and Tactics*: 'I have seen a Persian horse 14 hands 3 inches carrying a man of our regiment (15th Hussars) of gigantic proportions and weighing in marching order twenty-two and a half stone: I have seen this horse on the march ... of 800 miles carrying this enormous weight with ease and keeping his condition well'. Even as late as 1876, Troop Sergeant-Major Mole, of the 14th Hussars, claimed that, of the assortment of Arabs, Kandaharis, country-breds and Cape horses on which his regiment was mounted, 'the Arab-bred came nearer to perfection in symmetry, beauty, temper and performance than any horses I have ever seen, and they were soon snapped up as chargers by our officers'.

In addition to Arabs and country-breds, the South African Cape horse was for long highly regarded as a remount in India, and vast numbers were imported during the first half of the nineteenth century. The Cape was the descendant of the first horses brought to South Africa by the Dutch settlers in the seventeenth century, with later crossings of Arab and Thoroughbred blood. The equine species had become extinct in that part of the African continent before the emergence of man, and those Dutch horses were the first to be seen by the natives.

The Cape horse stood higher than the Arab—often 15 hands—and possessed equal stamina. Colonel Valentine Baker, of the 10th Hussars, preferred him above all others; his own Cape charger, Punch, which had formerly belonged to Sir Harry Smith, carried him throughout the Kaffir War of 1851–3 and the Crimean campaign before being brought home to England. 'This horse has done extraordinary work since he has been in my hands, yet his legs are as fresh as a foal's. He is always in good condition and is very good tempered, and though an entire, is perfectly quiet to ride, even amongst mares. He has accompanied me on eight different sea voyages, and is a first-rate sailor.'

During the late 1830s the Cape breed was so highly thought of that Lord Auckland, Governor-General of India, presented a pair of stallions to the Sikh leader, Ranjit Singh, as a token of British friendship; whether 'the Lion of the Punjab' was impressed is not recorded. When his armies fiercely opposed British rule in the Sikh wars of the 1840s, his horsemen were well mounted on their own little Punjabi horses. Ranjit's personal charger, which had helped him to carve a Sikh empire in Northern India, was a remarkable grey stallion. Kabutar (Pigeon) long outlived his master and was at least thirty-five years old when inspected by Lieutenant W. C. Mcdougal of the HEIC Stud Department in 1858. He had become a great pet of the Sikhs 'who treat him with the greatest kindness and are loud in his praise'. The veteran, 14.1 hands, was described as being 'now as fat as possible', and no wonder; his daily diet was 'two-and-a-half pounds of sugar, two-and-a-half pounds of fine flour, and one-and-a-half pounds of clarified butter (ghi), besides sweetmeats of all sorts. He can neither eat grain nor grass'.

The Indian Army remount which eventually superseded both the Cape and the Arab was the Waler from Australia. He was a descendant of the original horses brought by the colonists to what became New South Wales—hence his name—and evolved from Thoroughbred, Arab and Cape blood. A few Walers had been bought for British regiments in India during the 1850s, but it was not until after the Mutiny that they became popular and completely ousted the Cape. The British cavalry regarded them as ideal troop horses, for they were the big 15–16 hand type of mount they had been accustomed to at home; they had good paces and could keep going without tasting corn. More powerful than both Arab and Cape, they soon became almost the regulation type for the horse artillery. Out of 900 remounts purchased for cavalry and artillery in 1881, no fewer than 771 were Walers; the remainder were country-breds (69) and Arabs (60). In World War I, Australia sent 121,324 Walers to India, the Middle East and France.

By the middle of the nineteenth century, stallions had ceased to be acceptable as troop horses in Europe, but in India the battle of the sexes continued to occupy the authorities. In 1850 the C-in-C, General Sir George Berkeley, ordered a 'scientific' test to determine the relative stamina of stallions and geldings. With equal proportions of each, the 15th Hussars and the Madras Cavalry were subjected to a 'forced march' of some 400 miles. Captain Nolan, riding with the 15th, observed that 'they brought in but one led horse; stallions and geldings did their work equally well, and were in equally good condition on return'. On this test, the troopers and sowars were not in full marching order, but rode 'light', averaging a mere 14 stone. Sir George decided in favour of geldings; besides being more docile to handle, they were reported somewhat surprisingly, to 'require less food'.

Nevertheless, in the 1890s, the uncut troop horse was still causing some unmilitary diversions on parade. When the 7th Hussars arrived at Mhow in 1891 they took over Arab and Gulf stallions, and 'the squeals, rearing and kicking that went on during assembly in the half-light of the early mornings were both vulgar and dangerous', as Major-General John Vaughan wrote in his *Cavalry and Sporting Memories*. Sergeant Burridge, of the 5th Royal Irish Lancers, reported in his manuscript diary that the stallions received in India were 'an eye-opener from our home mounts'. If any broke loose on exercise, 'there was hell to pay . . . these loose horses not only attacked any spare horse wandering around, but they would jump on the back of your own mount'.

Service in India in the nineteenth century was tougher than anything the British soldier experienced elsewhere. His ranks were ravaged by cholera, dysentery and malaria, and in each major campaign or 'punitive' operation the sheer physical strain and the hot climate caused as many losses as enemy bullets. The misconceived and mismanaged Afghan War of 1839–42 is chiefly remembered for the humiliating evacuation of Kabul and the utter defeat of an entire British force. But, reading accounts of the operation, one wonders how the 'Army of the Indus' ever succeeded in reaching the Afghan capital in fighting trim. On the seventeen-day march over the Bolan Pass to Kandahar, in April 1839, one Troop of Bombay Horse Artillery lost seventy of its 169 horses through exhaustion and want of forage. The Troop records paid tribute to the remarkable endurance of their Cape and Persian (Arab) animals, but 'all the low-bred country horses were killed off by the privation and hard work'. In the same march 190 horses of the 16th Lancers died or had to be destroyed, and by the time the invading force reached Ghazni in July, 1,500 'public cattle'—horses and pack mules—had succumbed. This is not surprising, for during much of the period rations had been cut to 1lb of grain per day instead of the usual 10lb. The men existed on 1lb of *ata* (maize flour) and whatever else they could find 'off the country'. After the frozen snow of the Bolan, came the roasting heat of the Afghan plains, which took further tolls. On one April day seventy horses of the British and Indian cavalry died from exhaustion. Colonel Thackwell, commanding the 16th Lancers, wrote in his diary that the hardships 'have completely ruined this fine cavalry, and will reduce us to a state of starvation'.

The occupation of Afghanistan ended with the annihilation of some 16,000 troops, families and camp followers during the terrible retreat from Kabul in January 1842. The news of the disaster was brought to the British base at Jalalabad by Dr William Brydon, the only one to escape slaughter or capture. The well-known painting by Lady Butler shows the solitary horseman slumped in the saddle of his mount, the exhausted animal being scarcely able to carry him to the gates of the fort. In a recently discovered letter*, written shortly after his arrival at Jalalabad, Brydon described how he had taken over the horse from a wounded officer within 50 miles of the fort. It had an Afghan saddle, so it may well have been seized from an enemy casualty. In the final mêlée, Brydon 'ran the gauntlet for about two miles under a shower of large stones, sticks and shots, in which I had my sword broken, my horse shot in the spine close to the tail ...', he himself being wounded in leg and hand. Eluding the last of their pursuers, the two survivors struggled the remaining 20 miles to collapse at the gates of the fort; Brydon was 'quite done up, as also my poor horse, who lost the use of his hind legs and died two days after, without even getting up after his arrival'.

In the Second Afghan War of forty years later Lord Roberts is said to have been carried by his favourite charger, Vonolel, through not only two years' campaigning but also on the famous forced march of 320 miles in twenty-one days, from Kabul to Kandahar, in 1879. 'Vonolel' was so called in commemoration of the general's successful expedition against the Lushai chief of that name on the eastern frontiers of India in 1871. A pure-bred Arab stallion from the desert, he was imported to Bombay by the Indian horse-dealer Abd-al-Rahman, from whom

the military authorities bought large numbers of animals in the 1870s and 1880s. Lord Roberts purchased Vonolel in 1878, when he was said to be a three-year-old, but this seems a remarkably tender age to undergo the gruelling conditions of active service in Afghanistan—particularly as a C-in-C's first charger. As these imported Arabs had no documented pedigrees, it is likely that the alleged foaling date of 1875 was inaccurate. The animal was a grey, standing about 14.3 hands, and fully up to the general's weight, for he rode only 10 stone.

If 'Bobs' cherished any feeling for his charger, he did not make it public. In his two-volume autobiography, *My Forty-One Years in India*, published in 1897, there is not a single reference to the horse which, by that time, had become almost as celebrated as his owner. However, on leaving India in 1893, Lord Roberts brought Vonolel home with him and, in 1897, to the delight of the crowds, rode him behind Queen Victoria's carriage in the Diamond Jubilee procession. On his breastplate Vonolel wore the Kandahar Star and Afghan medal, presented by the Queen herself. When he died two years later the old war horse was given a military funeral and was buried, appropriately, in the military pensioners' cemetery in Dublin.

Equally entitled to honours is another Afghan War veteran, Maidan. He was a pure-bred Arab stallion, bought from Abd-al-Rahman in 1871 by a Captain Johnstone of the Indian Army, who raced him as a three-year-old, with some success. In 1873 Johnstone sold him to Lieutenant-Colonel F. Brownlowe, commanding the 72nd Highlanders, who was a big man, riding 19 stone; as his charger, the 14.3 hh Arab carried him faultlessly throughout the Afghan campaigning and on the Kabul–Kandahar march. When Brownlowe was killed in the final battle of

* *Journal of the Society for Army Historical Research* LI, 207 (Autumn 1973).

A bullet was the only kindness to a wounded horse in the field. This picture by R. Caton Woodville shows an incident in Afghanistan, 1882

Kandahar, Maidan passed to Lord Airlie and, in his fourteenth year, was bought by Captain the Hon Eustace Vesey of the 9th Lancers.

Posted home in 1885, Vesey took his charger with him and, making a detour to Pau in the Pyrenees, raced him against the fine Arabs of the French Government stud. When Vesey died a year later, his executors sold Maidan to Miss E. Dillon, of Charlbury in Oxfordshire, who founded one of the earliest Arabian studs in England and was among the first exporters of pure-bred Arabs to the USA. The old stallion, still virile and active, sired a number of fine animals, including Jamrud, which became one of the most sought-after Arabian sires of his day; his name is to be found in several English, American, Dutch and Spanish Arabian pedigrees. At the age of twenty, Maidan won many point-to-points against Thoroughbreds, and at twenty-two he won a three-mile steeplechase. A year later, in 1892, this noble survivor of the Kabul–Kandahar march broke his leg and was sadly put down at Charlbury.

Of the many celebrated cavalry actions in the nineteenth century, none has inspired so much admiration—and condemnation—as that of the charge of the Light Brigade at Balaclava, in October 1854. Never before or since have mounted troops performed such an incredible feat of sheer courage and discipline—which by all the accepted rules of warfare should have been impossible.

The Light Brigade consisted of the 4th Light Dragoons, 8th Hussars, 11th Hussars

13th Light Dragoons, and 17th Lancers.* None of these regiments was up to strength; earlier casualties and the usual wastage of horseflesh at sea and during the previous six months had reduced them to little more than squadron strength. The 8th Hussars were down to 104 all ranks, and Lord Cardigan's entire command mustered only 673 men and horses. All had been shipped from home the previous spring, and the English-bred horses were in poor shape after their unwonted privations and shortage of forage. The day before Balaclava a sergeant of the Lancers wrote: '. . . it is pathetic to see how our poor animals have fallen off: mine is more like a costermonger's nag than a Lancer's mount'.

The action took place in a completely open, level valley nearly 1½ miles long and varying between 700 and 1,000 yards in width. At the far, or eastern, end was the brigade's (mistaken) objective—a Russian battery of twelve 12-pounder guns supported by some 3,000 cavalry. To the north, the valley was overlooked by the Fedioukine Heights, on which were posted eight battalions of Russian infantry, four squadrons of cavalry and eight field guns. The south side was enclosed by the Causeway Heights, defended by two infantry battalions and twelve guns.

With their muzzle-loading weapons, the enemy infantrymen and gunners could get off about two or three rounds per minute. The brigade's advance—the actual charge—down that swept zone of some 1,000 yards took approximately ten minutes, and the withdrawal about the same, with a further ten minutes or so spent in the mêlée around the gun position. The volume of projectiles that must have been hurled at the mass of men and horses during the twenty minutes or so when they were exposed to its full fury leaves one incredulous that there were any survivors. As an officer wrote afterwards: 'There is only one explanation— the hand of God was upon us.'

Before the Brigade had advanced more than 400 yards there were scores of riderless horses which could well have saved themselves by galloping anywhere out of the inferno, but they did not. Lord Paget, among others, described how, even though terribly wounded, the horses strove to keep their places with the rest 'as though their masters were on their backs', causing no little confusion by trying to force themselves into the ranks. At one moment, seven of them were crowding in on Paget himself 'covering my overalls with their blood', and he was obliged to belabour them with the flat of his sword to clear a passage for his own mount. Private Wightman of the Lancers saw a comrade blown out of the saddle by a shell-burst; the riderless grey mare continued to gallop alongside him until, to his horror, he saw her stumble and fall, with her legs entangled in her own entrails.

The first shell to strike the Brigade killed Captain Nolan, and his horse, still bearing the bloody corpse, bolted to the rear through the oncoming ranks. Later it was found galloping back up the valley among the ranks of the 13th Light Dragoons, to be seized and mounted by one of their sergeants who had been unhorsed. It was finally killed under the muzzles of the Russian battery.*

The Light Brigade horses were reacting in the way an experienced horseman would expect them to in such circumstances—they were obeying primitive instinct. Though by nature timid, the horse is intensely gregarious; if alarmed,

* Represented today by: The Queen's Royal Irish Hussars (4th and 8th); The Royal Hussars (10th and 11th); 13th/18th Royal Hussars; 17th/21st Lancers.

* This horse was identified by Nolan's own saddlery and cloak, now to be seen in the National Army Museum.

he will seek safety in flight, but his herd instinct is uppermost and wherever the herd goes he will strive to follow—even into the cannon's mouth.

The horsemanship of the Light Brigade troopers was extolled by a correspondent in *Horse and Hound* some years ago; he maintained that only superb riders could have kept their mounts going straight for those guns. But, as subsequent letters pointed out, the horses needed no urging, and little guidance; launch a body of horses into a gallop, and if one leads the rest will surely follow—come shot, shell or rifle bullet. In this case the leader was the flashy chestnut Thoroughbred, Ronald, who bore the Brigade commander, Lord Cardigan, straight into the smoke of the guns and back again with, miraculously, no more than a scratch from a lance-thrust.

Far from having to 'leg' their horses forward, the men were constantly restraining them, and had it not been for the unshakeable parade-ground discipline— 'Look to your dressing there! . . . keep back on the right flank! . . .'—the ever-decreasing formed ranks would have scattered into penny packets of individuals in a mad race. Captain White, commanding the 17th Lancers, was greatly embarrassed when, tug as he might, his over-impetuous charger committed the sin of drawing level with his Brigade commander, and the shocked Lord Cardigan had to restrain him with the flat of his sword and a sharp reproof.

As in other cavalry actions, it was remarkable how even mortally wounded horses kept going until they dropped. Lieutenant Sir William Gordon of the 17th owed his life to his charger. In the skirmishing among the Cossacks in rear of the gun position he was severely wounded by sabre-cuts on head and neck, while his mare received a deep lance-thrust through the shoulder. She carried

him, clinging round her neck, almost a mile back to the spot where the attack had been launched, then collapsed and died, with blood pouring from mouth and nostrils.

The charge of the Light Brigade may have been a criminal and costly blunder— '. . . n'est pas la guerre'—but it achieved its objective, smashing through the Russian guns and so demoralising their cavalry, already mauled in the lesser-known charge by the Heavy Brigade, that they were virtually discounted for the rest of the campaign. Of the 673 all ranks who went into action at Balaclava, 113 were killed and 134 wounded; 470 horses were killed, 42 wounded and 43 put down 'as unserviceable' after the action. As some historians maintain, in twenty minutes Lord Raglan had destroyed the Light Brigade.

The remnants—together with all the other British horses, cavalry and artillery —were to suffer even more from the rigours of the ensuing winter and the shocking apathy of the administrative departments in the Crimea. Ex-Rifleman George Evelyn wrote in his diary: 'The enemy . . . had indeed destroyed the greater parts of our cavalry, but really in so doing he had given himself a deal of unnecessary trouble. The exposure and privation would have done it for him far more effectively'. Seemingly, it did not occur to the commissariat that English horses picketed out in the extremes of the Crimean winter required food and clothing. Major Phillips, of the 8th Hussars, wrote in November: 'The last two weeks have been wet and cold. They have told severely on the horses; having had no hay the poor brutes are desperately hungry, and at least ten horses have lost their tails in consequence: they have literally been eaten off. Some horses have lost their manes also'. By December the whole of the Cavalry Division (Light and Heavy

Lord Cardigan on 'Ronald' encounters Russian
Lancers at Balaclava

The Crimean War: the Charge of the
Light Brigade at Balaclava, after C. Clark

Brigades) had been reduced from their original strength of 2,000 to no more than 200. A month later the 13th Light Dragoons could muster only twelve of the 250 horses they had brought from England—and these were so wretchedly poor that they could not be ridden out of a walk.

This melancholy picture is painted by a correspondent to *The Illustrated London News* of 3 February 1855:

I noticed one horse in particular: it was the most pitiful sight I ever beheld. Once upon a day he had been a handsome charger, but now he was the veriest caricature ... a skeleton covered with an old hide; no mane, no tail; deep-set ghastly, glaring eyes, and lips shrunk away from the long hungry teeth. You could not tell the colour; his hair was covered with a thick coat of mud which fitted him tight, like a slush-coloured leather jerkin ... There he stood, shivering in the sun, up to his knees in mire, tied to what had once been a shrub, but now was a bundle of withered, leafless sticks. Sterne wept fictitious tears over the carcass of an ass that lay by the roadside. He would have wept real tears— as many stronger and better men have done—if his *Sentimental Journey* had brought him to our Cavalry Camp.

No more than a handful of the British horses ever saw England again. Of those that did, Lord Cardigan's gallant Ronald naturally became the idol. Not at all averse to publicity, Cardigan basked in the hero's reception accorded to him after his return, and whenever he appeared mounted on Ronald the crowds surged forward and tried to pluck hairs from the horse's mane and tail. He was an eye-

Field-Marshal Earl Roberts, vc, on his Arab charger Vonolel, from the painting by Charles Furse

catching Thoroughbred, standing 15.2 hands, his deep rich chestnut coat shown off by contrasting white legs. He had been bred by Cardigan at his country seat of Deene Park, near Corby, in Northamptonshire, and he returned there to spend his last years in well-earned retirement.

In March 1868 Cardigan was thrown from his horse and died shortly afterwards. It has been said that he was riding Ronald, but this is not so; his mount was a young fresh animal which, as friends had warned him, was hardly suitable for the ailing seventy-one-year-old warrior. Ronald followed his master's coffin to the grave at Deene, where he was greeted by several 'Balaclava Officers' of the 11th Hussars, who had come to pay their last respects to their old colonel. The horse lived on until 28 June 1872, when he was put down and buried at Deene—all except his head, which was mounted and placed under a glass case in the entrance hall of the manor house, where it surveys the tourists who flock there in the summer months.

A more humble equine survivor of the Light Brigade was Old Bob, later known as Crimean Bob; a troop horse, he was, like the Brigade commander, an ex-11th Hussar. This old soldier commenced his career in the 15th Hussars (Nolan's regiment), was transferred to the 14th and then to the 11th, when he became the farrier-major's mount and was ridden by him throughout the Crimean campaign. Never known to be sick or sorry, Old Bob not only survived the Balaclava charge but also the rigours of that Crimean winter, and returned with his regiment to Britain. He died aged thirty-four at Cahir, County Tipperary, in 1862, and was buried with full military honours by the regiment, who also erected a tombstone to his memory.

The War Horse in the States

The Spanish colonisation of the southern portion of the North American continent took place during the mid-sixteenth century, when De Soto reached the Mississippi and Coronado's army penetrated the plains of Kansas. The primitive savages they encountered—the 'Indians' —were the descendants of migratory tribes who, thousands of years before, had come questing out of the steppes and across the land-bridge that existed over the Bering Sea—the same bridge that had enabled the primeval equine herds to migrate in the reverse direction. At first overawed by the mounted conquistadores, these tribes soon discovered that horse and man were not a single animal, and that the strange 'elk-dog'

From old drawings of Cortés fighting the Indians. They are here burning the temple of the idols

yeqtla ti tetzavitl yn mal ques.

could be tamed by any human, including themselves.

The Indians saw that the horse could transform their order of life, giving them unprecedented mobility and allowing them to hunt down the herds of buffalo on which they depended for their meat. By 1700 all the great tribes of the Missouri, the Kiowas and the Comanches, had become skilled horsemen, and within another ninety years the northernmost tribes were their equals. Many of their animals were acquired from the Spanish colonists, either by raiding or by barter, while some were captured from the herds of wild *mesteños*, or mustangs, which were now roaming the plains. But it was not long before they were breeding their own stock, and soon an Indian's wealth, and his family, were dependent on the number of horses he owned.

Superb horsemen though they were, the Indians were never noted for their horsemastership; they had no sentimental feelings for their domesticated animals, dog or horse. Mark of prosperity or not, the horse was no more than a means of mobility and a weapon of war; if he became a casualty he could easily be replaced. Writing of the 14-hand Indian 'cayuse', in *Our Wild Indians*, Colonel Dodge of the US Army records that his endurance was incredible. He was never stabled, seldom groomed and seldom fed; when not ridden he was turned loose to fend for himself, and in winter would perish if the squaws did not gather branches of cottonwood for him to pick. No mercy was shown to him under a saddle: 'An Indian will ride a horse from the back of which every particle of skin and much flesh has been torn by the ill-fitting saddle, ride him at speed till he drops, then force him to his feet and ride him again'.

There was an old Western saying that an American would abandon a horse as broken down; a Mexican would then mount and ride him 50 miles further; an Indian would then mount and ride him for a week.

The horse transformed the Indian tribes into a nation of mounted warriors whose tactics and prowess equalled those of the Mongols. It was the horse that enabled them to hold out against the advance of the white man for nearly a century, but before they came to grips there were other conflicts to attend to. In the War of Independence, which shook off British dominion and saw the creation of the American nation, the horse played a very minor role. The 'rebels' could field only a few ad hoc troops of so-called 'Horse' and dragoons; the British had two regiments, the 16th and 17th Light Dragoons. Because of the terrain and paucity of good horseflesh, neither side was able to display much cavalry spirit.

When South Carolina led the way to civil war by seceding from the Union in December 1860, there were, according to official statistics, 6 million horses in government and private ownership throughout the United States. Of these, quite a high proportion were fine well-bred types, including breeds which have since become famous: the Morgan, the Quarter Horse, the Saddlebred, all with Thoroughbred and Arabian blood, and there were also large numbers of mustangs, chiefly from Texas. On the outbreak of the Civil War in 1861, and for the next couple of years, the Confederates enjoyed the advantage in horseflesh and cavalrymen. The Southern planters and farmers were born horsemen, riding to hounds like their English equivalents, at home with sporting gun and rifle, proud of their own studs, never walking when they could ride. Nearly all the best breeds were located in the Southern states, which included the famous Blue Grass country of Kentucky (though this State did not

The American War of Independence: gathering of the mountain men at Sycamore Shoals

formally join the Confederacy until 1862). The Confederate cavalry used to boast that 'every horse, like its rider had a strain of gentle blood'.

The spirit of the 'Reb' cavalryman was summed up by Private Mosgrove of the 2nd Kentucky Regiment, who declared that all he needed was 'a good horse, a Mexican saddle, a pair of big spurs with bells on them, a light long-range gun, a brace of Colt's revolvers, a good blanket, and a canteen of brandy sweetened with honey. When he had these things, or some of them, he was a merry fellow, ready to dash into battle . . .'

The Yankees of the North were largely urban in occupation and outlook; they used the horse mainly for draught and the plough rather than the saddle. They had, however, a useful heavy artillery and transport animal in the Norman, which was descended from Percherons imported in the previous decade. The Southerners scoffed at these beasts, 'as wide as a barn door and slow as molasses', and laughed at the idea of riding one into battle.

It was generally conceded that the best

type of cavalry mount was the Saddlebred, formerly known as the Kentucky Horse, of which the Confederates had the greater proportion. Colonel Basil Duke of the 2nd Kentucky Cavalry ('Morgans' Raiders') claimed it was '. . . very valuable for cavalry service because of other reasons than merely his superior powers of endurance. His smoother action and easier gaits render a march less fatiguing to the rider; he succumbs less readily to privations and exposure, and responds more cheerfully to kind and careful treatment. He acquires more promptly and perfectly the drills and habits of the camp and march, and his intelligence and courage make him more reliable on the field'.

Later, Major-General C. L. Scott, of the US Cavalry, wrote of his Saddlebred mare: 'I thought nothing of riding her forty miles a day on a march, and then driving her fifteen or twenty miles in harness at night.' Small wonder he 'never expected to own a better, all round useful horse'.

The American Civil War was the world's first major conflict since Napoleonic times and brought about a revolution in cavalry tactics. The American trooper had always disliked the sabre and scorned the lance, putting his faith more in the carbine and rifle; and the European 'heavy cavalry' concept, with its traditional fetish for the *arme blanche* and implicit belief in the battering-ram effect of shock action, was never adopted in the States. While there were some notable massed cavalry charges, as at Brandy Station, the cavalry of both Federal and Confederate forces functioned essentially as mounted infantry—as the US Cavalry regiments were to do later against the Indians. It was not until the British confronted the elusive Boer farmers in South Africa that these tactics gained any currency outside America.

In the Civil War the basic principle of cavalry tactics can be summed up in the words of that dashing Confederate leader, General Bedford Forrest: 'Git thar fustest with the mostest.' The mobility of your horse was your weapon; and when you got there you didn't wave your sword and get shot to pieces; you dismounted, saved your horses, and gave the enemy better than you received.

Whereas the regular cavalry of the Federal forces were supplied with government mounts, the Confederate officers and men brought their own with them on enlistment, the authorities providing forage and shoes—in theory at least, for both were soon in woefully short supply. If a horse was killed, the Conferedate government paid a valuation to its owner, who was then responsible for finding another. This system (which had its parallel down to 1922 in the *Silladar* cavalry regiments of Britain's Indian Army) worked well enough in the early stages of the war. But as the conflict dragged on, with its toll of horse casualties from sickness and malnutrition, it was almost impossible for a dismounted trooper to find a remount. Even if he did, he could not afford to buy it, for the average

market price had increased to about $2,000 by 1864, and the government allowed him only the impressment price of $500. The law was changed the next year, but by then it was too late.

Acute shortage of horseflesh had bedevilled General Robert E. Lee throughout his campaigns. By the fall of 1864 more than a quarter of his cavalrymen were dismounted, and several artillery units were unhorsed. A veterinary hospital had been established in the Lynchburg area in October 1863, but it was of little avail; animals were sent there only when they were so exhausted that recovery was rare. By February, out of 6,875 horses admitted, 2,844 died, 599 were condemned and cast, and 1,483 were still unserviceable. In March 1864, Lee was writing despondently to Jefferson Davis: 'Unless the men and animals can be subsisted, the army cannot be kept together, and our present lines must be abandoned...' Within a month Lee surrendered at Appomattox. It would be facile to claim that the outcome of the Civil War was decided by horseflesh; but the want of it was certainly a contributory factor.

The Federals had started the war with only six regular regiments—most of which were hardened Indian campaigners—but by 1863 the number had risen to thirty-six, with a total strength of some 14,000. They too had their horse problems; it was calculated that three remounts were needed for each man every six months. While the 'Rebs' of the South used whatever saddlery, and weapons, they could lay their hands on, there was naturally more uniformity in the Federal regiments, and one item was to prove a tried veteran. In 1858 General George B. McClellan had introduced to the US Cavalry a new, lightweight pattern of saddle, based on the Prussian–Hungarian type he had observed on his European travels. This was patented in 1865, and the 'McClellan saddle' remained the regulation pattern throughout the US Army until horsed units were abolished in 1942; it also found its way to the British cavalry and mounted infantry in the Boer War.

One of the more common, cold-blooded ordeals which horses had to undergo in war was when a battery's gun-teams had to stand patiently enduring enemy fire. A most revealing description of their reactions to such circumstances is given by a Union artilleryman of the Army of the Potomac, John D. Billings:

The best illustration of the fortitude of horseflesh that I ever witnessed occurred on the 25th day of August, 1864, at Ream's Station, on the Weldon Railroad. In this battle the 57 horses belonging to my company stood out in bold relief, a sightly target for the Rebel sharpshooters who, from a wood and cornfield in our front, improved their opportunity to the full. Their object was to kill off our horses, and then by charging, take the guns if possible.

It was painfully interesting to note the manner in which our brave limber-horses—those which drew the guns— succumbed to the bullets of the enemy . . . A peculiar dull thud indicated that the bullet had penetrated some fleshy part of the animal, sounding much as a pebble does when thrown into mud. The result of such wounds was to make the horse start for a moment or so, but finally he would settle down as if it was something to be endured without making a fuss, and thus he would remain until struck again. I remember having my eye on one horse at the very moment when a bullet entered his neck, but the wound had no other effect on him than to make him shake his head as if pestered by a fly. Some of the horses would go down when hit by the first bullet, and after lying quiet awhile would struggle to their feet again, only to receive additional wounds . . .

When a bullet struck the bone of a horse's leg it made a hollow snapping sound and took him off his feet. I saw one pole-horse shot thus, fracturing the bone. Down he went at once, but all encumbered as he was with harness and limber, he soon scrambled up and stood on three legs, until a bullet hit him vitally. It seemed sad to see a single horse left standing, with his five companions all lying dead or dying around him, himself the object of a concentrated fire until the fatal shot laid him low. I saw one such brute struck by the seventh bullet before he fell for the last time. Several received as many as five bullets, and it was thought by some that they would average that number apiece . . . Long before the serious fighting of the day occurred, but two of the thirty-one nearest the enemy remained standing. These two had been struck, but not vitally, and survived some time longer. We took but four of our fifty-seven horses from that ill-starred fray.

(*Hardtack and Coffee*, 1888)

To horse gunners of a later generation it would have seemed criminal stupidity to allow a battery's sole means of mobility to be systematically destroyed, with no attempt to find cover. But, as at Waterloo, it was still the regulation drill for gun-teams to be posted within immediate 'limbering-up' distance of their guns, with utter disregard of the consequences. Commenting on the horse's powerful herd instinct, Billings adds that it was sad to witness a crippled horse attempting to hobble along and keep up with the column.

In April 1861 Thomas J. 'Stonewall' Jackson, then a colonel, had command of the Confederate post of Harper's Ferry, where one day his Virginian volunteers were fortunate in capturing an east-bound train en route for Washington. Truck-loads of Western horses, destined for the Federal cavalry, were gleefully seized by the Southerners. Inspecting the windfall, Jackson, who had no personal charger, selected a useful-looking big sorrel geld-ing. Another smaller animal, also sorrel, took his eye; this seemed an ideal lady's hack which would make a welcome present for the devoted Mrs Jackson, and accordingly he purchased the two. After trying both he found that the big sorrel had uncomfortable paces and a somewhat hard mouth, whereas the smaller, though not handsome, was all that a good saddle-horse should be. So the unwitting Mrs Jackson lost her gift-horse and the lady's hack became a general's charger. The big sorrel was passed on to Jackson's chaplain, the Rev Beverley Lacy, a worthy Presby-terian minister who feared neither man, devil nor hard-mouthed beast. Jackson named his new mount Fancy, but since he and his chaplain were constantly to-gether, their grooms preferred to identify the smaller animal as 'the little sorrel'.

Little Sorrel was barely 15 hands high, a Western of uncertain breeding and, according to Henry Kyd Douglas who served on Jackson's staff, 'was a plebeian-looking little beast ... stocky and well-made, close-coupled, excellent legs and feet ...' He showed remarkable en-durance and was always a good doer: 'he would eat a ton of hay, or live on cobs'. Jackson himself was no polished horseman: 'walking or riding, the General was ungainly ... he rode boldly and well, but not with grace or ease; and Little Sorrel was as little like a Pegasus as he was like an Apollo'. General Jackson was astride his little charger at the first great victory of Bull Run in July 1861, when another Confederate general admired Jackson's brigade, 'standing like a stone wall'—and thus bestowed a *nomme de guerre* which was to become inseparable from his name.

Throughout the ensuing Valley cam-paign, Little Sorrel served his master faithfully, until in May 1863 'Stonewall' Jackson was fatally wounded at Chan-cellorsville. This was also the end of the little sorrel's campaigning, for the Gover-nor of Virginia presented him to the general's family, and the next twenty-odd years of his life were spent peacefully on the farm of Mrs Jackson's father, the Rev R. H. Morrison, in Lincoln County, North Carolina. There he became a family pet. Old Fancy, as Mrs Jackson always called him, discovered the knack of manipulating stable door-bolts with his lips; he not only set himself free but would perform the same service for the other horses in the yard.

In his old age the veteran was cared for, appropriately, in the Confederate Soldiers' Home at Robert E. Lee Camp, Richmond, where he died on 16 March 1886, at about thirty-five years of age. His stuffed hide was displayed for many years at the Camp Museum, and the skeleton was on view in the Carnegie Institute, in Pittsburgh, Pennsylvania, but later both were handed over to the Virginia Military Institute, Lexington, where they are still to be seen. The lifelike stuffed figure carries a British army saddle and bridle, presented to General Jackson in 1862 by an English admirer, Lieutenant-Colonel James Freemantle of the Coldstream Guards.

If Little Sorrel was of common stock, General Robert E. Lee's famous Traveler was an aristocrat. A big 16-hand, well-made iron-grey gelding ('Confederate grey', as Lee described him), he was more than half Thoroughbred and had in him the blood of Black Hawk, one of the most celebrated of the early Morgan sires. He was bred in 1857 by a gentleman-farmer, James Johnston, near Blue Sulpher

General Robert E. Lee on his charger Traveler. This horse was his constant companion throughout the Civil War, and followed him into retirement. The skeleton is now preserved in the Washington and Lee University, Lexington

Springs, West Virginia; as a colt, with the name of Jeff Davis, he took first premium at the Greenbriar Fair. Lee was not only a fine horseman but a good judge of horseflesh; as soon as he saw Jeff Davis as a four-year-old in the spring of 1861, he bought him, changing his name to Traveler—possibly because General Grant although a loyal Unionist, also had a horse called Jeff Davis. Until the general's death nine years later, the horse was his constant companion in war and peace. Lee wrote to a painter friend after the Civil War: 'If I were an artist like you, I would draw a true picture of Traveler, representing his fine proportions, muscular figure, deep chest and short back, strong haunches, flat legs, small head, broad forehead, delicate ears, quick eye, small feet, and black mane and tail ...' Lee went on to detail Traveler's service during the war: the Seven Days' Battle around Richmond, Second Bull Run, Sharpsburg, Fredericksburg, Chancellorsville, Gettysburg, and the final surrender at Appomattox. For the last few weeks of campaigning 'the saddle was scarcely off his back'. He was never wounded, despite four years' constant active service, and is said to have been remarkably calm and manageable under fire.

After the capitulation, the fifty-eight-year-old general, honoured and respected by friend and foe alike, was given the presidency of Washington College, Lexington, and Traveler went with him. For the last five years of his life, the horse was his 'only companion; I may say, my only pleasure'. He rode him every afternoon, and personally took him to the blacksmith when his feet needed attention.

The old horse became a privileged character at Lee's house, and was allowed to wander at will in the garden and shrubbery—to the dismay of the gardeners. Shortly after Lee's death in October 1870, Traveler stepped on a nail; tetanus followed, and there was no alternative but the bullet. The skeleton is now preserved in the Washington and Lee University, Lexington.

Another Civil War veteran which eventually ended up in a museum was Winchester, General Philip Sheridan's charger. He came of good stock, having Black Hawk blood in him, and was a most impressive-looking animal: standing over 17 hands, he was deep black in colour, with powerful quarters, deep girth, and a fine head. Foaled at Grand Rapids, Michigan in 1859, he was only a three-year-old when Sheridan acquired him. Originally named Rienzi, the horse was called Winchester to commemorate Sheridan's ride from the town of that name to the battle of Cedar Creek in 1864. After the war the general submitted an official record of his charger's services:

> ... He was brought into the service by an officer of the Second Michigan Cavalry, to which Regiment I was appointed Colonel, on the 25th day of May, 1862. Shortly afterwards, and while the Regiment was stationed at the little town of Rienzi in the State of Mississippi, he was presented to me by Captain Campbell in the name of the officers ... and from that date until the close of the war he was ridden by me in nearly every engagement in which I took part ... He was an animal of great intelligence, and of immense strength and endurance. He always held his head high, and by the quickness of his movements gave many persons the idea that he was exceedingly impetuous. This was not so, for I could at any time control him by a firm hand and a few words, and he was as cool and quiet under fire as one of my old soldiers. I doubt if his superior as a horse for field service was ever ridden by anyone.

Sheridan appended a list of forty-seven engagements at which Winchester was present—from Perryville in October 1862 to Appomattox in April 1865.

On Winchester's death in 1878 Sheridan had the body stuffed and mounted, and presented it to the Military Service Institution, Governor's Island, New York. Later it was transferred to the Smithsonian Institution, Washington, where it is displayed to this day, with the general's original saddlery, in the Hall of Armed Forces History.

Henry Kyd Douglas, of 'Stonewall' Jackson's staff, recalls in his memoirs the sad death of his mount, Dick Turpin, at Cedar Creek. The horse had been slightly wounded in the leg when a rifle bullet plunged into his lower jaw. 'He gave a weird cry of pain and sprang into the air, then he reared straight up and, throwing his head back in agony, struck me in the face and knocked me from the saddle.' Remounting, Douglas managed to urge the wounded animal into a supreme effort; with blood pouring from his mouth and spattering his rider, he galloped through an enemy column and, in the dark, negotiated a deep ravine to bring Douglas to safety among his own troops. As soon as they halted the horse collapsed. 'I took the bit gently from his mouth, and when he lifted up his head in pain and tried to rub it against me in mute appeal for help, it seemed to me that tears were gathering in his eyes: but it may be they were those in my own. Two days afterwards he died of lockjaw.'

In the decade after the Civil War, the Indian Wars of the American Frontier reached their peak. Scattered in isolated posts across some 2½ million square miles from the Mississippi to the Pacific, the US Army forces—seldom more than 3,000 strong—were constantly pursuing, fighting, and being slaughtered by 200,000 of the world's most adept and ruthless guerilla horsemen. And for sheer cold-blooded savagery the Apache, the Cheyenne, the Comanche, Kiowa and Sioux were unequalled. 'Forty miles a day on beans and hay in the Regular Army O!' sang the soldiers of the West; on campaign, the days usually amounted to months, in the snow and sub-zero temperatures of the High Plains or the gruelling heat of the southern deserts. 'A pretty fair summer's campaign' was how George Howard of the 2nd US Cavalry summed up, after being out for eight months and, in the saddle for 2,600 miles. The men were as tough as any legionnaire of the Sahara, and as cosmopolitan; the Irish brogue was as common as the American twang in the ranks, while German and Italian accents ran it close.

The ten regular regiments of cavalry were mounted on a mixture of horseflesh, with Morgan, Saddlebred and Thoroughbred blood predominating. The Arab which would have vied in hardiness with the Indian pony, was never used in fighting the Indians and was not in fact bred in any large numbers in North America until the close of the nineteenth century. The cavalry horses, of at least 15 hands, were grain-fed on the longest marches; the horsemastership was generally good, and performance under trying conditions was usually better than anything European, cavalry could show. Yet time and again the Indians, on their undersized, scrubby-looking *cayuses* could outdistance the blue-coats and elude pursuit. Their superior mobility was in the main due to their *remuda* system; whereas the US cavalryman was limited to a single horse throughout a campaign, each Indian rode a dozen or so in turn, the spares being herded along by the boys of the tribe. While the trooper's horse was laden with all the regulation impedimenta, plus rations for man and beast, the Indian's unshod pony lived off the country, as did his rider.

Tough and hard-bitten though the frontier troopers may have been, most of them could evince the true cavalryman's feeling for his horse: 'I found that Sam was shot in the bowels . . . and I had to shoot him to end his misery. I had to try two or three times before I could do it: he kept looking at me with his great brown eyes. When I did fire he never knew what hurt him. He was a splendid horse . . .'

The only Indians said to have cherished any depth of regard for their horses were the Nez Percé tribe of the North West. Alone among the tribes, they developed their own breed of animal, which was later to become popular far outside their territory. The Appaloosa, or 'Spotted Horse', took its name from the fertile Palouse district bordering the Snake River, the original homeland of the Nez Percé.

Although there were many better soldiers and abler leaders among the Indian fighters—George Crook and Phil Sheridan, for instance—it was the flamboyant George Armstrong Custer, 'the Boy-General' of the Civil War, 'the Glory-Hunter' of the Frontier, who achieved a controversial immortality equalled only by that other colourful cavalryman, Lord Cardigan of the Light Brigade.

On 25 June 1876, General Custer and his 7th Cavalry attacked, unsupported, a force of some 3,000 Sioux and Cheyenne warriors on the Little Big Horn River in southern Montana. The outcome was the most shattering defeat ever suffered by

General Grant with his favourite bay charger, 'Cincinnati'

American soldiers at the hands of the Indians. Custer and his immediate command of five troops were annihilated, and the remainder of the dispersed regiment were so mauled that they would have met the same fate had not a relief column arrived with timely intervention. Of a battle strength of 600 all ranks, 263 were killed and 44 wounded, while 319 horses perished.

'Custer's Last Stand' made an emotional impact on the American public similar to that of Balaclava on the British, and aroused as much heated controversy; but the Little Big Horn disaster was no Light Brigade charge. It was not, strictly speaking, a cavalry action at all, for Custer and his subordinate commanders dismounted their men at the outset, and attempted to fight it out on foot with their Springfield carbines and Colts. In this they were merely conforming to US Cavalry custom in the Indian wars, when there were few mounted charges and little use of the sword. But, if Custer and his men had not gone down in a blaze of glory at the Little Big Horn, the most famous of all American war horses would never have been heard of outside his regiment.

When the relief column arrived, they found, among the carnage of dead horses and stripped and mutilated bodies, one buckskin gelding still on his feet. He was the sole survivor. Blood oozed from wounds in his flanks and neck; the headstall of the bridle had been severed and the bit hung out of his mouth; the saddle had slipped under his belly. Lieutenant Henry Nowlan recognised the animal as the charger of his friend and fellow-Irishman, Captain Myles W. Keogh, whose naked body he had just identified.

Captain Keogh was one of many Irish soldiers of fortune who had fought with the Papal Zouaves—as did Nowlan—and later sought adventure in the American Civil War. Emerging as a brevet lieutenant-colonel, he then joined the newly-raised 7th US Cavalry under Custer and was given command of 'I' Troop as a substantive captain. In June 1868, when the regiment was stationed in the field near Fort Leavenworth, Kansas, Keogh selected a personal charger from a bunch of forty remounts just arrived from St Louis. His choice was a six-year-old buckskin (light bay) of 15 hands, with a small star on the forehead and a white near-hind fetlock. Keogh paid the regulation price of $90 for him and never regretted the purchase. He had easy paces, was quiet to handle, and showed remarkable stamina on the gruelling campaigns in which the 7th were perpetually engaged. In his first baptism of fire—a skirmish with the Comanches at Bluff Creek, Kansas—the horse received an arrow in his quarters, but stoically carried his rider for the rest of the fight with the broken shaft still in the wound. Back in camp he patiently allowed the farrier to extract the steel head, and in recognition of his courage on that day, Keogh named him Comanche.

How Comanche came to survive the Little Big Horn is a mystery; every other horse had either died from Indian bullets and arrows or had been shot by its rider, to serve as a breastwork. The braves usually carried off any surviving animals for their own use.* Perhaps they judged this one as good as dead.

The first reaction of the relief force was to put him out of his misery, but Farrier Gustave Korn thought the horse might have a chance; he and other troopers of the 7th Cavalry resolved that this solitary living representative of their regiment's fight should be taken back to

* They did capture some unwounded horses, but none found their way back to the 7th Cavalry.

'Custer's Last Stand,' Little Big Horn, 25 June 1876

Comanche, only survivor of Custer's immediate command at the battle of the Little Big Horn

regimental headquarters. They dressed his wounds and, with men supporting him on each side, Comanche was led painfully the 15 miles to the mouth of the Little Big Horn River, where the steamer *Far West* was waiting to evacuate the casualties. Bedded down under an awning on the after-deck, his welfare became the concern of the whole ship's company during the record-breaking fifty-one hour trip downstream to Fort Bismark. From there Comanche was transported to the 7th's base at Fort Abraham Lincoln, and for nearly a year remained on the sick list, supported by slings in the veterinary hospital. He had suffered twelve wounds from bullet and arrow in flanks, neck and quarters; the miracle is that none had touched a vital organ.

Comanche was fully recovered when,

in April 1878, Colonel Samuel D. Sturgis, commanding the Regiment, issued the following order:

Headquarters, Seventh U.S. Cavalry, Fort Abraham Lincoln, Dakota Territory, April 10, 1878

General Orders No. 7

1. The horse known as "Comanche" being the only living representative of the bloody tragedy of the Little Big Horn, Montana, June 25, 1876, his kind treatment and comfort should be a matter of special pride and solicitude on the part of the 7th Cavalry, to the end that his life may be prolonged to the utmost limit.

2. The Commanding Officer of "I" Troop will see that a special and comfortable stall is fitted up for Comanche. He will not be ridden by any person whatever under any circumstances, nor will he be put to any kind of work.

3. Hereafter upon all occasions of ceremony (of mounted regimental formation) Comanche, saddled, bridled, and led by a mounted trooper of Troop "I", will be paraded with the regiment.

By Command of Colonel Sturgis
(signed)   E. A. Garlington
1st Lieutenant and Adjutant
7th US Cavalry

This order, which is claimed to be unique among all armed forces, was faithfully complied with for the rest of Comanche's life. He was allowed complete freedom of the regimental lines: 'Front lawns and flower gardens meant nothing in his life. His stamp of approval was to be found on every garden, and sunflowers were a special diet to him.' Naturally, the fame of this 'Second Commanding Officer of the Garryowens' spread throughout the USA, and the Regiment was constantly receiving tempting offers from showmen and others anxious to cash in on it; to the 7th's credit, all were spurned.

Comanche died 'from colic and general debility' at Fort Riley, Kansas, on 6 November 1891, aged twenty-nine. His body was mounted and put on display in the Museum of Kansas University, at Lawrence, and in 1893 was exhibited in the Chicago World Fair.

Nearly a hundred years after his ordeal on 'Custer's Hill', Comanche survived another brush with his old enemies. Under the headline 'Stuffed Horse stays at KU', *The Denver Post* of 25 April 1971 reported that some Indian students at Kansas University were agitating to have Comanche removed from their museum and sent back to the military post at Fort Riley. They claimed that the old warrior was a 'racist symbol', commemorative only of the white man, and they objected to the notice describing the horse as 'the only survivor'; some Indians also survived that battle, they pointed out. But the Indians lost their second 'Little Big Horn'. The university authorities, backed by State officials, decreed that Comanche should remain undisturbed, where his regiment had bequeathed him, and there at Kansas he can still be seen in his glass case.

Patient Eyes, Courageous Hearts

The twentieth century brought in motorised transport and the heavier-than-air flying machine. Methods of warfare were revolutionised by the infantry's automatic machine guns capable of firing 800 rounds a minute, with a range of 2,000 yards; their rifles were magazine-fed, accurate to more than a mile, and the new 'quick-firing' field guns enabled the artillery to put down devastating concentrations with 12 and 15lb high-explosive shells.

All these developments were ignored, no less by dedicated cavalry leaders than by the majority of military minds in Europe. Cavalry in all its traditional glory was still 'the arm of the gods'; oats, not petrol, were the fuel of mobility, and mounted shock action was the true function of the horseman. In Britain, the official view was reflected by the 1907 issue of

British hussars in South Africa, 1890

115

Cavalry Training which categorically asserted: 'It must be accepted in principle that the rifle, effective as it is, cannot replace the effect produced by the speed of the horse, the magnetism of the charge, and the terror of cold steel.'

The Franco-Prussian war of 1870–1 had produced some magnificent charges of massed squadrons in the style of Frederick the Great, by both sides. At Vionville, von Bredow's brigade smashed through the enemy artillery and virtually halted the advance of the French 6th Corps. Right down to 1914 this was cited as proof that a classic cavalry charge still had its effect on the modern battlefield. It was conveniently forgotten that only 420 of von Bredow's 800 troopers survived the charge. At Sedan, five French regiments of chasseurs and hussars gallantly charged the Prussian infantry and within fifteen minutes were virtually destroyed. Said an observer: 'It was a useless, purposeless slaughter ... the hillside was literally covered with their dead and the bodies of their little grey Arab horses'. One regiment had only fifty-eight all ranks left out of the 216 that galloped into action.

In peacetime cavalry brigades, resplendent in their outmoded extravagance of full dress, presented a magnificent spectacle as they marched past in review order. This was an occasion of brilliant pageantry, with some 1,500 hussars, lancers and dragoons in scarlet, blue and gold; the glint of sword-steel and lance points, fluttering pennons; the jingle and clink of bit and curb chain, and clash of sword scabbard and stirrup iron, and the thunderous drumming of hooves. Above all, there was that almost sensual thrill afforded by rank after rank of glistening horseflesh, muscles rippling beneath sealskin-like coats, proud heads tossing, silken tails swishing.

Obstinately, Britain and the other European powers refused to glance across the Atlantic at the exemplar of the United States cavalry, and when, in 1899, British horsemen landed in South Africa they were dismayed to find themselves hopelessly outmatched by 'gangs of bible-thumping Boer farmers on scraggy little ponies'. The Boers were essentially mounted infantry and their hardy little Basuto horses, seldom bigger than 14.2 hands, were capable of covering 60 miles a day on little more than the grazing they could find on the veldt.

Initially, the British cavalry and artillery units shipped out their own English- or Irish-bred horses; the sea voyage to the Cape took their toll of them. Lieutenant Lord Blackwood, 9th Lancers, described in a letter to his father the fearful havoc wrought by a storm encountered in the Indian Ocean on 10 October 1899:

... At length the rolling became terrific and the seas enormous. The wooden framework of the stalling began to crack and I expected every minute to see the whole thing collapse and all my men killed ... Five minutes after that one entire side of the woodwork gave way. Two of my chargers and 4 others were at once washed overboard. Now came the most horrible scene I have ever witnessed. The deck was covered with one struggling mass of horses and mules, mixed up with the broken woodwork of the stables, the whole being hurled first to one side of the deck and then the other. All were horribly wounded, most with broken legs and some with eyes torn out. My first charger (the one you gave me, and the nicest horse I am ever likely to have) was amongst them, but I managed to get a shot at her with my revolver, and so I am glad to say none of my three suffered the torments of hell like the others ... Things were hardly better between decks. On one deck, a huge

water tank broke loose and went hurtling about, killing two horses . . .

Charge of 21st Lancers at Omdurman, 1898, by E. M. Hale

In twelve hours the regiment lost seventy-one troop horses and twelve officers' chargers.

On arrival, there was no time for acclimatisation, and there followed the inevitable ravages by disease and exhaustion. After less than one year in South Africa the 9th Lancers could parade only thirty-six horses out of the 518 with which they had started the campaign. In the last phase of the war the Queen's Bays (2nd Dragoon Guards) lost no fewer than 748 of their 775 troop horses and chargers —mostly from disease and privation.

At home, in the ordered routine of barrack life and on the not-too-arduous formalities of annual manoeuvres, the British trooper's horsemastership was probably as good as any other's. But peacetime training gave him no experience of caring for underfed, overloaded and hard-pushed animals, in a country where oats and hay were not available at every halt, and often remote from vets and farriers.

A desert-bred Arab stallion standing 14.3 hands, Bashom was ridden in the charge of the 21st Lancers at Omdurman. He was brought home to England and acquired by the Hon Mrs Ives of Morpens Park, Essex, who used him to sire many fine polo ponies

Lord Lovat, who raised and took out to South Africa the yeomanry regiment later known as Lovat's Scouts, reported in 1901 that out of 100 remounts issued by the remount department 'thirty-five had strangles or parasitic mange and 11 had both strangles and mange. Eight horses had pink-eye [influenza] and there were, between mares that had foaled, old sore backs opened and horses kicked in the box, no more than a dozen fit for work . . .' The final casualty figures for the four years of the Boer War were appalling: 350,000 dead out of a total of 520,000 remounts supplied from the remount departments at home and in South Africa. Giving evidence before a commission after the war, Major-General Brabazon confessed that he 'never saw such a shameful abuse of horseflesh in the course of my life . . . I was shocked: I was horrified'.

At Ladysmith and Mafeking many fine

English horses had been slaughtered to feed the beleaguered garrisons. 'It gives one something to think about,' wrote a 5th Lancer officer in Ladysmith, 'being one of a brigade of British cavalry suddenly turned into infantry and order to eat their own horses.' In Mafeking almost every part of the dead animal was put to use: mane and tail went to the hospital to stuff mattresses and pillows; shoes to the foundry for making primitive round-shot; flesh was finely minced and stuffed into portions of intestines to produce 'sausages'; bones were first boiled to extract all nutriment for soup—'chevril'—and then pounded up to mix with flour. The skin was boiled, with head and feet, chopped up small, and served as 'brawn'.

The memory of the thousands of horses which perished in the Boer War of 1899–1902 is perpetuated by an impressive statue in Port Elizabeth, Cape. At one of the busiest street junctions, the life-size bronze figures form an eye-catching feature above the modern traffic. Surmounting a stone drinking trough, a British soldier kneels to offer water to his exhausted horse. The plinth bears the inscription:

> The greatness of a nation
> consists not so much in the number of
> its people
> or the extent of its territory
> As in the extent and justice of its
> compassion

The memorial was the idea of Mrs Gustav Meyer—formerly Harriet Bunton, of King's Lynn, Norfolk—who lived in Port Elizabeth. She organised a public subscription in 1904 and £800 was quickly raised, one of the principal donors being the London Metropolitan Drinking Trough Association. The sculpture was carried out by Joseph Whitehead and unveiled in February 1905.

In 1910 an ex-yeomanry trooper who had served in the Boer War published a book, *War and the Arme Blanche*, which aroused a storm of controversy among die-hard cavalrymen. Erskine Childers had already achieved some celebrity with his novel *The Riddle of the Sands*, in which he forecast the German naval threat. To the fury of horsemen in high places this one-time, amateur private soldier turned scribbler* had the temerity to proclaim that the sword was 'as dead as the dodo' and the only justification for retaining the horseman in war was to turn him into a mounted infantryman, relying exclusively on the rifle. His claims were based not only on the lessons of the Boer War but also on those presented by the United States cavalry.

By this time most military thinking agreed that there was a case for providing the cavalryman with effective fire-power in the form of rifle and pack machine gun, and in training him to fight dismounted 'when occasion demanded'; but the old school maintained, in the words of the official *Cavalry Training*, that 'the moral effect of a mounted attack with sword or lance remains as great as ever . . .' Thus, if never quite sure of their true role, cavalry clung obstinately to the *arme blanche*, and continued to dream of that ultimate thrill, the charge in line.

In the armed forces of Europe, cavalry and field artillery had evolved into a pattern which was to remain virtually unchanged until mechanisation. With the dream of shock action always present, the cavalry demanded the big, weight-carrying horse of at least 15.2 hands. In Britain the hunter type, preferably with Thoroughbred blood, had become the regulation stamp. The Indian Army continued to

* Erskine Childers turned to Irish politics and died before a British firing squad; his distinguished son, of the same name, was President of the Republic of Ireland when he died in 1974.

Royal Artillery crossing river under fire in
South Africa, 1900, by George Scott

Edwin Noble's drawing of a horse ambulance
in World War I. Each mobile veterinary
hospital section was supplied with an ambulance,
mainly out of subscriptions raised by the RSPCA

German transport horses with 'horsepirators' in World War I

favour the Australian Waler, although government stud farms were also producing useful country-breds with English blood. On the Continent, the French preferred their *demi-sang* (half-bred) Norman breed—a heavy cavalry type of 16 hands or so, while the Germans put their faith in their excellent Trakehner and Hanoverian animals.

Thanks largely to Federico Caprilli, the Italian cavalry officer, who introduced the so-called 'forward seat' in the early 1900s, military horsemanship had shaken off the straitjacket of over-collection, and that 'tongs across a wall' seat with long leathers and straight leg. Caprilli claimed that 'manège and cross-country equitation are, in my opinion, antagonistic: one excludes and destroys the other'—a precept that is echoed by many modern hunting folk.

In civilian circles, the rising trot had superseded the 'bumping' or sitting trot during the early part of the previous century, but its adoption by the soldier was long frowned upon. Since it is not possible to persuade a squadron of horses to trot 'in step' on the same diagonal with identical strides, the spectacle of men bobbing up and down 'out of time' was considered untidy and unsoldierlike; and so horses' backs and soldiers' posteriors suffered in the name of smartness. It was not until 1876 that the rising trot was permitted in the British mounted service, and then only on non-ceremonial occasions. To this day, the Household Cavalry and The King's Troop RHA are to be seen 'bumping' through the streets on their ceremonial duties.

The problem of 'weight on horse' continued to be a source of controversy and was never resolved; when the British cavalry took the field in 1914 their mounts were still burdened with an average of 22 stone. More than half this weight was made up by saddlery, arms, ammunition and the plethora of equipment, clothing and 'comforts' considered necessary for a mounted soldier on service. This was the regulation Field Service Marching Order outfit:

On the man
Clothing, including spare boots, braces, cap, drawers, field dressing, great coat, cap comforter, socks, jacket S.D., knife, pantaloons, puttees, shirt, cardigan, 'housewife', towel, respirator, bandoleer (with 90 rounds S.A.A.), water-bottle, mess tin, haversack, one day's rations.

On the horse
Saddlery (with spare blanket), rifle in bucket, sword and scabbard (and lance for Lancer regiments), groundsheet, nosebags (with one day's feed), surcingle pad, picketing pegs, heel rope, picketing rope, grooming kit, spare shoes in case, canvas water-bucket, wallets, horse bandoleer (90 rounds S.A.A.), wire cutters, spare change of clothing for man.

In Europe the conflict of 1914–18 was essentially one of trench warfare, dominated by machine gun and artillery. Although there were a few gallant cavalry actions with the *arme blanche* in the early days, the cavalryman soon reverted to the original dragoon role of mounted infantryman, his horse being useful only to move him quickly from one part of the line to another. Nevertheless, on the allied side at any rate, generals—who were mostly cavalrymen—continued to be obsessed with the dream of an ultimate 'cavalry breakthrough', and vast numbers of troop horses were kept in the field awaiting the chance that never came. In 1916, when the world's first tanks dismayed the Germans, there were more than one million cavalry horses on all fronts—the largest mass yet assembled for war.

The inherent glamour of the cavalry horse has always tended to overshadow the noble and no less essential services of those thousands of draught-animals on which the armies in France and Flanders were almost entirely dependent for the movement of their guns, and the supply of ammunition, rations and all other matériel necessary to maintain troops in the field. In World War I all but super-heavy 'position' artillery was horse-drawn; there were six horses to each field gun, eight or twelve to the medium and heavy types, and each gun had its supporting ammunition wagons. It was reckoned that on any sector of the front between 1916 and 1918 there was one gun for every ten yards of the line; the number of horses involved is incalculable.

The sufferings of the animals were occasioned more by privation than by battle casualties; out of 256,000 horses lost by the British forces in Europe, only

David, gun-team horse of 107 Battery RFA. Served in Boer War and throughout World War I. From a painting by Lucy Kemp Welch

58,000, or less than a quarter, were destroyed by enemy action. The chief cause of horse wastage was officially given as 'debility'; this was brought about not by shortage of rations as in other campaigns, but by exposure which lowered the animals' resistance. Picketed out in the open in the Flanders winters, often standing in liquid mud over the fetlocks, even the hardiest 'good doers' rapidly lost condition and succumbed to lung and digestive troubles. During the winter of 1916 a single veterinary hospital in France was losing an average of fifty horses per week through a virulent form of influenza.

Generally, the standard of horsemastership throughout the war was higher than in any previous campaigning, but sometimes the efforts of the men in the field were frustrated by authority. There was

In Field Service Marching Order the British cavalry troop horse of 1914–18 carried an average of 22 stone

A pack horse in difficulties on the Western Front

the problem of clipping, for instance. If a horse is to be worked hard in winter he must be clipped, or his heavy winter growth of coat will cause undue sweating and distress, besides making proper grooming difficult. But the clipped-out horse is not, as in wartime, tethered in the open and exposed to the elements with nothing but a sodden blanket over him. Nevertheless, the regulations in 1914 were: 'clip out' in November and, said Colonel A. G. Arbuthnot of the Royal Artillery, 'it cost us the lives of hundreds of horses and destroyed the remnants of condition of the remainder'. Some unit commanders used their own discretion: the battery commander of 'C' RHA ordered all grooming kit to be dumped on landing at Ostend and clipping was forbidden: 'The horses' coats grew thick and strong and were waterproofed by all the grease left

in the hair, so that although they stood in the open all that very hard winter, none died and we had very little sickness.' Grooming was reduced to scraping off the mud with the men's canteen knives and rubbing down with hay or straw. It was not until the final year of the war that the happy mean of trace clipping— removing hair from legs and belly only, leaving back and loins naturally protected —was officially approved.

On active service the rapport between man and horse developed to a degree seldom attained in peacetime, when— except on manoeuvres—the trooper or gunner saw his horse only on daily 'stables' and mounted parades. Very often he did not ride the same animal on two consecutive days and his barrack room was usually out of sight and sound of the horse lines. On campaign, riding and tending the same horse for months on end, sleeping in the open only a few yards behind

The Battle of Pilckern Ridge. Pack mules
passing wrecked artillery limber and dead mules
at St Jean, 31 July 1917

the picket lines at night, and suffering
the same privations, the soldier came to
regard his horse as almost an extension
of his own being. Perhaps the equine
species is incapable of any true, dog-like
affection for man, but this has never
prevented the reverse. There are many
stories from the Western Front of strong
men in tears over their stricken mounts.

A painting by Matania was very
popular in the immediate post-war years.
Entitled *Goodbye Old Man*, it showed an
artillery driver kneeling to nurse the head
of his dying team-horse, while in the
background one of his mates in the
advancing battery impatiently beckons
him to stop his nonsense and rejoin the
column.

Mawkish artistic sentiment? Not so;

while writing this book I received a letter
from an ex-troop sergeant of the 19th
Hussars, describing an incident which
might have served as a model for that
picture. During a withdrawal under fire
in May 1918,

> ... I was riding with the Squadron
> rearguard when one of the troop horses
> was badly hit by MG fire. Horse and
> rider crashed down in front of me. The
> horse lay on its side and the trooper,
> unhurt, had rolled clear. Kicking one
> foot out of the stirrup, I ordered the
> trooper to mount behind me. Instead,
> he crawled towards his horse which
> had raised its head and was looking at
> him. He reached the horse, gently lifted
> its head on to his knees, and stayed put.
> I again ordered him to mount, and
> drew my pistol, saying I would shoot
> the animal. He said nothing; just
> looked up at me, then down to the

'Goodbye, Old Man', after F. Matania (see p. 129)

horse, and continued to stroke its head. From the look in the horse's eyes, I think it knew it was the end, and I also think it understood its master was trying to give it what comfort he could. I didn't shoot. Bullets were still smacking around and the squadron was almost out of sight. I said something to the effect 'Well, it's your funeral' and trotted on to rejoin my place. The trooper caught up with the squadron later: he had stayed with his horse till it died. By all the laws of averages, he should have stopped one too.

A new and devilish weapon on the Western Front was gas. Although this inflicted serious human casualties, there was surprisingly little loss among the horses. Between 1916 and 1918 there were only 2,220 equine casualties from gas, of which a mere 211 died. The first

The Battle of Ypres: a water cart stuck in mud near St Eloi, 11 August 1917

Northamptonshire Yeomanry crossing a stream in Italy

gas masks for horses—'respirators, gas, horse'—issued by the British Army were regarded as a joke, as indicated by an ex-artillery correspondent: '. . . Just a damn great flannel bag tied with tapes behind the horse's ears. The snag was that our horses were always fed with nosebags, so anything looking like a nosebag and pulled over their heads should logically contain oats: horse sense. Bag tied on, down went head, and horse rooted around trying to find the oats that weren't there. Soft flannel bag: life expectation as a gas mask, three minutes flat'. Horses were found to be much more resistant than men to the effects of chlorine and mustard gas, but the latter type was a severe skin and eye irritant, causing most of the equine casualties.

World War I was the first major European conflict in which properly organised veterinary services took the field. In Britain, the mounted arms had had to make their own arrangements for all veterinary matters until, in 1881, the Army Veterinary Department was formed, the regimental system abolished and the army assured of an efficient service with professionally qualified veterinary officers. In 1914, for the first time in history, sick and wounded horses could be evacuated to field and base hospitals where they received treatment comparable with that given to their human comrades. During the four years of the war, 2,562,549 horses and mules were admitted to British veterinary hospitals in France; of these, 78 per cent or nearly 2 million were cured and returned to duty. The devoted services of the Army Veterinary Corps (as it had then become) were acknowledged by King George V in November 1918, when he conferred upon it the prefix 'Royal'.

THE GREATNESS OF A NATION
CONSISTS NOT SO MUCH IN THE NUMBER OF ITS PEOPLE
OR THE EXTENT OF ITS TERRITORY
...JUSTICE OF ITS COMPASSION

The Horse Memorial in Port Elizabeth, South Africa

If the war in France offered few opportunities for 'the cavalry school!' to justify its dogged faith, General Allenby's victorious campaign against the Turks in Palestine showed that, given the conditions, the horse—and the *arme blanche*—could still play a decisive role in modern warfare. The Desert Mounted Corps of some 20,000 Australian, New Zealand, British and Indian cavalry and mounted infantry was the largest force of horsemen ever to operate tactically under one command in the war, and their achievements were remarkable by any standards. Marches of 60 miles a day were common; there was one instance of 90 miles in twenty-five hours, and in November 1917 the whole force advanced 170 miles in less than four days. All this was in the arid, waterless terrain of deep sand or rocky upland and, usually, in temperatures approaching 100°F. Moreover, all animals were carrying their normal marching order of at least 20 stone. In his *History of Horsemanship*, Charles Chenevix Trench describes how his own Indian regiment, Hodson's Horse, rode 56 miles in twenty-six hours, 'in great heat, fighting several stiff actions. Thirteen exhausting days later the regiment reached Damascus after a final day's march of 63 miles with negligible horse-wastage'. In this same advance the Berkshire Yeomanry Battery RHA covered 78 miles in thirty-six hours —'not bad going for guns,' as the battery captain modestly observed.

Apart from the enemy, water was the chief problem. Wells were few and far between, and often 150ft or more deep; the only method of watering the horses was to let down buckets on lengths of telephone wire. Thus it could take an hour or more to water the thirty-odd horses of a single troop.

In peacetime, it was the practice to water a cavalry horse four times daily; it was held that he needed about ten gallons a day in hard work, 'more in hot weather'. Nevertheless, a horse, unlike his mechanical successor, does not immediately seize up when he runs dry; he will survive just as long as his rider. In Palestine the animals of the mounted divisions frequently went waterless for fifty and sixty hours, at the same time marching up to 60 miles in severe heat. The record was achieved by the horses of the Worcestershire Yeomanry who survived ninety hours without a smell of water. Lord Cobham, in his history of the Regiment, wrote: 'Many of the animals were now in a bad state, as was only natural. But it was indeed a wonder that, coming as it did on the heels of a period of sixty hours without off-saddling, these four days did not dismount half the Regiment. The Veterinary Officer inspected the horses during the morning, and sent only about a dozen away to hospital . . .' It is doubtful whether this example of endurance has ever been surpassed on active service.

No regular cavalry saw service in the Middle East. The British elements of the Desert Mounted Corps were all Yeomanry and many of their horses which performed such, literally, yeoman service were those they had brought from Britain—hunters, half-bred cobs, a few Thoroughbreds (officers' chargers) and, surprisingly enough, a number of hackneys pressed into use for the Sherwood Rangers and Gloucestershire Hussars Yeomanry. The hackney, a showy, high-stepping carriage animal, had never been favoured as a troop horse, but, as reported in the *Official History of the Great War*,* at the conclusion of the campaign the Director of Veterinary

* *Military Operations. Egypt and Palestine*, vol 2, Part II (1930).

Services was surprised to find a number of the Yeomanry's hackneys at Aleppo, 'apparently twenty years old or more. Though in poor condition, these gallant old horses kept their gay carriage, and the fact that they had reached Aleppo convinced him, against his will, of their hardiness and fitness for war'. The Australian Waler proved his worth—a 'cut and come again customer' who seemed to thrive on hard work and short rations; besides the Anzac units, many of the British received Waler remounts in Egypt and Palestine. One trooper paid tribute to his mount who 'carried me faithfully all the way across the deep shifting sands of the Sinai Desert, through the deep black mud of the Plain of Sharon, over the Judaean mountains and down to Jericho, up again to the mountains of Moab and on to Amman. The miles must have mounted to thousands, and all the time, no matter how exhausted, no matter how thirsty—he often endured the heat for thirty-six hours without a drink—he was off in a flash if asked. He had the heart of a lion'.

The Palestine campaign of 1917–18 was the glorious swansong of the British horse-soldier; not only was it the finale for large-scale employment of mounted troops, but it was the last in which the cavalryman realised his cherished dream of the thundering charge with sword 'in line'. At Huj near Gaza, on 8 November 1917, three squadrons of the Warwickshire Yeomanry and Worcestershire Yeomanry, numbering eighteen officers and 172 other ranks, charged a Turkish position held by four battalions of infantry, three batteries of guns and several machine guns. They sabred ninety of the enemy, took seventy prisoners, and captured all three batteries. 'For sheer bravery the episode remains unmatched,' commented the *Official History*, and the action was long quoted as an example of the demoralising effect

Australian Light Horsemen watering horses at Ain es Sultan, Palestine

that could still be created by bold and resolute bodies of horsemen. This Balaclava-like charge was costly to the gallant yeomen: all the squadron leaders and seventy men were killed or wounded, and of the 172 horses which galloped the batteries only seventy-two survived.

Less than a week later, on 13 November the Buckinghamshire Hussars Yeomanry and Dorset Yeomanry charged a strong infantry position on the El Mughar ridge. The six squadrons advanced at a trot under heavy fire for 2,000 yards and then stormed the steep, rocky hillside. Here, as their horses were blown, two squadrons dismounted and went in with the bayonet, but the remainder gained the crest mounted. Their spoils were more than 1,000 prisoners, two field guns and fourteen machine guns, and several hundred of the enemy were slain by sword and bayonet. The six squadrons suffered six-teen officers and men killed and 114 wounded, and 265 horses killed. The heaviest equine casualties occurred with the dismounted squadrons of the Dorsets, whose led horses were easy targets; the dismounted men themselves suffered more than their comrades who remained on horseback throughout—proving once again that a cavalryman's best asset was the mobility of his horse.

With the occupation of Aleppo in October 1918, Allenby's advance reached its triumphant conclusion and the Turks sued for an armistice. It was a curious coincidence that the campaign, which owed so much to the horse and was the last full-scale mounted operation in British history, should end at a city founded by the Hittites. Nearly 4,000 years earlier, they had been among the first warriors to use the horse in battle; and, some 60 miles away at Alexandretta (or Iskanderum)—a day's forced march for the Desert Mounted Corps—the cavalry of Alexander the Great had won him his

The 13th Australian Light Horse passing
Gressaire Wood on 22 August 1918

'Action front!' From the drawing by W. B. Wollen for *The Royal Artillery War Commemoration Book*, 1920

first great victory over Darius, the King of Kings.

By 1919 all the surviving British yeomen who had helped to win Allenby's victory were back in their native shires. Lloyd George, while earlier inveighing against 'the ridiculous cavalry obsession' of the generals in France, now paid tribute to Allenby's horsemen; 'their contribution to the rout of the Turkish Army will always be quoted as a conspicuous example of the services which cavalry can render in war . . .' and their horses 'were as unbeatable as their riders'. But, to the lasting shame of the prime minister and his government, it was decreed that all those war-weary horses—some 20,000 of them, belonging to the Yeomanry and others— should be cast and sold off in Egypt. The reason given was lack of shipping space and the expense of transport home. Those who knew the Egyptians realised this was a sentence of protracted death in slavery. There were vehement protests, especially from Major-General Sir George Barrow, GOC of the Yeomanry Division, but to no avail. British soldiers may argue successfully with their country's enemies, but not with its politicians.

It was this General—a genuine horse-lover—who turned a blind eye when officers of the Desert Mounted Corps took their favourite chargers out into the desert and shot them rather than let them be sold into slavery. But it is not possible to shoot 20,000 horses 'sub rosa', and the great majority were duly sold to work in the streets of the cities, in remote villages, and worst of all, in the stone quarries. Always hungry, weak, over-loaded to a degree, lame, crippled, galled, ill-shod, frequently blind, suffering from perpetual thirst . . . tormented by flies . . . straining under the whip . . .*

.*For Love of Horses: The Diaries of Mrs Geoffrey Brooke.

How the British Government of 1919 repaid the horses that had carried Allenby's Desert Mounted Corps to victory. This one was found by Mrs Dorothy Brooke slaving in a stone quarry outside Cairo

Thus Britain said 'Thank you' to all those 'courageous hearts' which had served her so nobly. This was another of history's examples of the casual or callous way in which man accepts all that a horse has to give and, when his usefulness is over, abandons him.

In 1930 Brigadier (later Major-General) Geoffrey Brooke was appointed to command the Cavalry Brigade in Egypt and his wife went with him to Cairo. Dorothy Brooke was a devoted horse-lover, and had long been actively interested in animal welfare in England. She, like her husband, had been horrified by the sale of the old army horses, which she 'hated to remember, but could not forget', and soon after her arrival she set about locating possible survivors. It was due to the courage and pertinacity of this 'Florence Nightingale of the war horses' that the shameful deed of the politicians was redeemed in full measure. Although sixteen years had passed, she found several—half-starved drudges in streets and quarries—recognisable as British cavalry horses only by the 'broad arrow' brand on their quarters. Their owners would not allow them to be put down while there was work left in them. Some she bought out of her own pocket and had them mercifully put out of their misery, but there were hundreds more, and she could not afford to pay and care for such a herd. So she wrote a letter to *The Morning Post* in London, appealing for help. Within three weeks came a flood of cheques, postal orders, money orders, letters of encouragement, promises of help; these initial donations totalled £600, and the following mail brought the sum to over £1,000. During the next four years horse-lovers world wide subscribed £40,000 towards the old War Horse Fund, stabling was acquired, and veterinary attention provided.

Mrs Dorothy Brooke and some of the old British Army horses rescued from the streets of Cairo

By 1934 some 5,000 ex-army horses had been rescued; many were in such dreadful condition that they had to be destroyed—nearly all were over twenty years old—but the remainder were able to spend the last few years of their lives in peace and comfort. On her husband's appointment as Inspector-General of Cavalry in India, Dorothy Brooke reluctantly left Egypt, but before doing so she saw the foundation of a properly equipped Old War Horse Memorial Hospital, which later opened its doors to all sick and suffering animals whose owners could not afford, or were unwilling, to pay for treatment. For the next twenty years Mrs Brooke continued her active interest in the hospital and in the welfare of surplus British army horses in Egypt and elsewhere. In 1935 she obtained an assurance from the government that the cast horses of mechanised cavalry and artillery units would not be sold to foreign civilians under any circumstances, but would be humanely destroyed if they could not be brought home. Dorothy Brooke died in 1955; since 1961 her foundation has become widely known as the Brooke Hospital for Animals, Cairo, and as such continues its good work to this day.

Armageddon

Many thousands of horses had survived the carnage in France and Flanders to be brought home to England, but when, in June 1934, the organisers of the International Horse Show had the happy (if somewhat belated) inspiration of staging a Parade of Veteran War Horses at each session, it was only possible at short notice to trace twenty-five. Assembled from all over the country at London's Olympia, the veteran horses were accommodated in special stabling, and paraded every evening, carrying shabracques emblazoned with their battle honours. All were aged—the youngest twenty-four and the oldest thirty-two—and some were already well known.

Throughout World War II pack horses performed valuable service in terrain impassable for vehicles

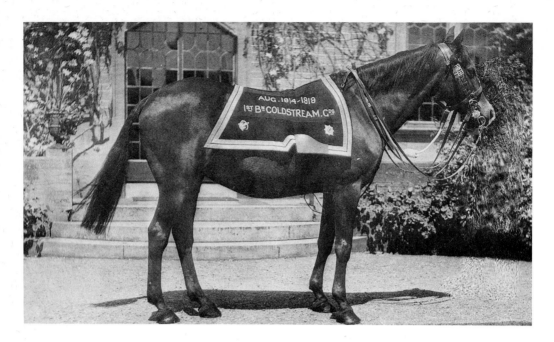

Kitty served throughout the First World War with the 1st Battalion Coldstream Guards. She is seen dressed for her appearance in the Parade of Veteran War Horses at Olympia, 1934

Londoners gave an enthusiastic welcome to Quicksilver—described as 'the best-known horse in London'; a striking 16-hand grey gelding, he was the personal mount of Colonel Sir Percy Laurie, Assistant Commissioner of the Metropolitan Police, and had appeared at every ceremonial function and parade since the Victory March of 1919. He had served throughout the war and was wounded by shrapnel on the Somme. There was Warrior, the charger of General Jack Seely (Lord Mottistone), which had carried Sir John French at the first battle of Ypres; he was later to become the most famous of all the war veterans with the publication of Lord Mottistone's book *My Horse Warrior*. The bay mare Kitty, belonging to Lord Digby of the Coldstream Guards, claimed the unique record of being the only infantry officer's charger to have gone through the whole war on the strength of one battalion and never to have missed a day's duty. Between the age of eighteen and twenty-two Kitty produced three foals; she was put down in 1940, aged thirty-one.

Others appearing at Olympia were four survivors of those gallant Desert Mounted Corps warriors whose comrades had been sold into slavery. One of the handful lucky enough to be brought home by their owners was Nigger; he had served with the Royal Buckinghamshire Hussars and charged with them at El Mughar. The other three were among those rescued from the Cairo *suqs* by Dorothy Brooke.

Most of the veterans applauded at Olympia were officers' chargers, but there were many others of humbler rank who missed the honour due to them. One of the most remarkable was David, wheel-horse in a gun-team of 107 Battery, Royal Field Artillery. When David went to France in August 1914 he was already eighteen years old and wore South African War ribbons on his browband. He helped to draw his battery's guns during the whole of World War I and was present at nearly all the major battles; he was never sick and was only once slightly wounded.

After the war, four officers of the battery clubbed together and bought him out, and his life ended peacefully in 1926 on the Hertfordshire estate of his former battery commander. He was then about thirty and was probably the last surviving horse to have fought throughout both the Boer War and the 1914–18 War.*

It was rare for a complete gun-team of six horses to remain together throughout the war, but this distinction was achieved by 'The Old Blacks' of the Royal Horse Artillery. They left St John's Wood Barracks, London, with 'J' Battery in August 1914, and after serving for the whole of the war returned to the same barracks in 1919, with two of their three original drivers. St John's Wood was the location of the 'ceremonial battery'—whose functions are today performed by The King's Troop RHA. The team of blacks drew the funeral gun carriages of many notable personages and on 11 November 1920 it was chosen to carry out this service in the funeral procession of the Unknown Warrior to Westminster Abbey. The grand old team was finally split up in 1926 when the horses were pensioned off, four going to an estate near Rugby and the other two to a farm in Kent.

Traditionally, Britain has been a nation of horse-lovers, but to her shame she has no national memorial to all those loyal and patient equine warriors who served and suffered in countless wars and helped to found the greatest empire in the world. In London's Hyde Park stands an imposing statue of St George slaying the dragon. Unveiled with appropriate pomp and ceremony in 1924, this Cavalry War Memorial was subscribed for by all cavalry units of the British Empire, whose titles are inscribed on the plinth; but

there is no mention of the horses that carried them. At the unveiling ceremony before a gathering of royalty, cavalry generals and 400 representatives of British, colonial and Indian mounted troops, Field-Marshal the Earl of Ypres made a fitting speech extolling the deeds of 'our gallant comrades who have given up their lives for their King and Country'. But he did not make a single reference to those equally gallant animals without which cavalry could not have existed.

The 1930s saw the advent of mechanisation. 'The cavalry lobby' could not, or would not, admit that the armoured fighting vehicle must sooner or later supersede the horse as the cavalryman's mount. Much of their argument stemmed from rooted sentiment and tradition; only the horse, they claimed could, foster those qualities of boldness and initiative that were as essential to a cavalryman in the field as to a foxhunter across country—in Britain, at any rate, 'the image of war without its guilt' was long held to be one of the finest forms of training for a soldier. The die-hards pointed out that the mechanical vehicle could not live off the land; the lessons of the Palestine campaign were quoted to show that even the sword could still be used with effect, and that some types of terrain were virtually impassable for wheeled or tracked vehicles though easily negotiable by horsemen.

In 1935 Hitler appointed Colonel-General Heinz Guderian to command the 2nd Panzer Division. Guderian was in no doubt about the future role of cavalry; its spirit and characteristics would remain unaltered, but the flesh-and-blood mount would be exchanged for one of steel. Within six years he was to lead his new-style armoured cavalry in their blitzkrieg conquest of Europe. Nevertheless, in the 1930s Germany foresaw some use for the horse, if only in a reconnaissance and transport role, as did all the other Euro-

* Lieut-Colonel Wingate-Gray MC, who kindly supplied this information, is the last survivor of those four officers who bought David's discharge.

With sheen of horseflesh, jingle of harness, the gun-teams of The King's Troop Royal Horse Artillery walk past the saluting base

pean powers—except Britain. Despite the vociferous 'anti-mechanical' school, two regiments, the 11th Hussars and 12th Lancers, had been converted to armoured car units as far back as 1928—the first regular cavalry in the world to be completely mechanised—and in 1938 came orders for the mechanisation of all but the Household Cavalry and two regiments, The Royal Dragoons and The Royal Scots Greys, then serving in Palestine. A few yeomanry regiments were also allowed to keep their horses. Other armies had created armoured forces by raising new units; Britain formed hers by banishing the horse.

Pundits in the United States held that cavalry—mounted infantry—should co-operate with mechanised troops, and most of the cavalry regiments remained horsed until 1940. Since the horseman could not be expected to keep pace with a mechanised column in good going, the Americans evolved the 'Portee' system in which horses and men were transported in trucks until action was imminent or the going became unsuitable for vehicles. This curious form of 'mechanicalised cavalry', unique to the USA, had obvious drawbacks, not the least of which were the slowness of the bulky horseboxes and their vulnerability to attack.

World War II is usually regarded as the first major conflict in which the machine, both on land and in the air, entirely superseded the horse; certainly it was the first in which tactics were dominated by the armoured vehicle and by fighter and bomber aircraft, and the first to see infantry 'mechanised' and transported in carrier and truck—becoming, in effect, a modern version of the original mounted infantryman. But the

The 'Old Blacks' gun-team of the Royal Horse Artillery, who left St John's Wood Barracks in 1914, served together throughout the First World War, and returned to the same barracks in April 1919. They drew the funeral gun-carriage of the Unknown Warrior on 11 November 1920

horse continued to serve, in vast numbers and in varied roles, to the end of hostilities.

In 1939 the most determinedly cavalry-minded nation was Poland—the first to be over-run by Hitler's Panzers. On the outbreak of war only three of her forty-one cavalry regiments were mechanised; the remainder fought mounted to the bitter end. The horse strength of the cavalry and supporting horse artillery was 37,250, while in addition 49,000 horses were serving as draught animals in the artillery, infantry and ancillary arms. Poland's army thus went to war with a grand total of some 86,000 horses. These ranged from tiny 11-hand Carpathian ponies, used for drawing the two-wheeled heavy machine guns and carrying the pack radios of the signal corps, to excellent Arab- and Thoroughbred-blood types of 15–16 hands for the cavalry.

Stories of suicidal mass charges by Polish lancers against German armour are largely propaganda myths. Captain Zygmunt Godyn, secretary of the Polish Cavalry Association of London, states that the Poles fought mainly on foot 'and the horse served only to add mobility'. In addition to the sword, each trooper was armed with a 7.89mm Mauser carbine, and every regiment had its quota of heavy and light machine guns and 37mm anti-tank guns. The cavalry did put in some gallant charges against German infantry, but in every instance they suffered heavy losses. Dive bombers took a fearful toll; in September 1939 the Pomeranian Cavalry Brigade lost nearly 2,000 of its 3,000 horses in thirty minutes: 'the best horses in the world could not withstand the demoralising attacks of the Stukas . . . Along the road to Warsaw lay thousands of dead and dying Polish-Arab horses'.

In the House of Commons in March 1939 the Secretary of State for War was asked whether mechanisation of the cavalry had been too precipitate, and was he aware that Germany was busy buying up surplus British cavalry horses? In fact, while Britain was getting rid of the horse as fast as she could, the German

Ancient and modern in World War II. A mounted orderly delivers orders to the commander of an SP gun unit, Eastern Front, 1942

nation, which was to excel in armoured tactics, was building up its horse strength for the cavalry, artillery and transport of the Wehrmacht. The United States *Cavalry Journal* of July–August 1940 quoted 'from reliable sources' a total horse strength of 791,100 for the German army; of these, some 18,300 were cavalry mounts, the remainder in horse-drawn artillery, mounted reconnaissance squadrons of infantry divisions, and supply columns. (At the same period the US army was reported to have 9,000 cavalry horses).

Hitler's élite SS Corps of thirty-eight divisions included five cavalry divisions, among them the much publicised 'Florian Geyer' (8th SS Division) and one Hungarian division (33rd). In 1944 another two cavalry divisions were combined to form the 15th (SS) Cossack Cavalry Corps. This was composed of Russian Cossacks, who had fled before the advancing Red Army, and served under their own leaders and a few German senior officers; these Cossacks paid the penalty for their transfer of allegiance; after surrendering to the British in Austria in 1945, they were handed over to the Soviet authorities,

who executed the officers and despatched the remainder to Siberian labour camps.

Russia's use of the horse throughout the war was on a colossal scale far exceeding that of any other power. When Hitler launched his Operation Barbarossa in June 1941 the opposing Red Army deployed no fewer than thirty cavalry divisions and a number of independent cavalry brigades, all with their supporting horse-drawn artillery. In addition, some 800,000 horses were used for draught and pack purposes in the infantry divisions. All in all, some 1.2 million horses served the Russians in the greatest so-called 'mechanised' campaign the world had seen.

Wartime press photographs of gallant Russian cavalry charging with sabres aloft were undoubtedly staged for propaganda effect; but, although the Red Army trooper was primarily trained to fight dismounted, such actions did take place. Probably the last full-scale cavalry charge in history occurred in November

1941 during the German thrust on Moscow. Near the village of Musino, north-west of Moscow, the German 106th Infantry Division, supported by the 107th Artillery Regiment, were awaiting orders to advance, when they were astonished to see squadrons of horsemen debouch from a belt of wood on their front and approach at a gallop, 'stirrup touching stirrup, riders low on their horses' necks, drawn sabres over their shoulders'. At a range of 1,000 yards, the German guns, rifles and automatics opened a withering fire, and only a handful of thirty horsemen reached the position, to be mown down by a burst of machine-gun fire. In ten minutes, 2,000 horses and their riders of the 44th Mongolian Cavalry Division lay dead and dying in the blood-stained snow. There was not a single German casualty.

During that winter campaign in Russia the savagery of the fighting was matched by the severity of the climate. One December day a German recce patrol encountered a group of six cavalrymen literally frozen stiff. 'The horses themselves were like the horses on the plinths of equestrian statues—heads held high, eyes closed, their skin covered with ice, their tails whipped by the wind, but frozen into immobility.' The troopers were slumped forward in the saddles, hands still gripping the reins. The number of horses lost by both sides during Operation Barbarossa ran into hundreds of thousands. A horse may keep going after a Panzer has run out of fuel or is frozen up, but he cannot exist for long with nothing in his belly but straw from thatched roofs.

While the struggle for Moscow was being fought out, British cavalrymen saw their last active service on horseback; in 1940 the 1st Cavalry Division was formed in Palestine, comprising the eight remaining mounted Yeomanry regiments and a composite regiment of the Household Cavalry, together with horse artillery and signals. With their varied assortment of English horses, ranging from Thoroughbred chargers to stocky Exmoor cobs, they endured a trying winter trip across France to Marseilles in the *40 hommes 8 chevaux* railway trucks familiar to the troops in World War I.

On that journey Corporal Harrison, of The Sherwood Rangers Yeomanry, was in charge of a hunter which had belonged to the Duke of Portland, of Welbeck Abbey, where Harrison had been stud groom. As recorded in Major T. M. Lindsay's *History of the Sherwood Rangers in the 1939–45 War,* halfway across France the horse developed colic and was removed from the train at a small station. Stranded on the platform, in the middle of France, with a valuable suffering horse and apparently no veterinary aid available, Corporal Harrison could think of only one solution. Brushing aside the protests of the stationmaster, he locked his patient in the waiting room and hastened to the nearest estaminet; he returned with several bottles of brandy and locked himself in with his partner. Some time later man and horse reappeared; the former in good humour and the latter no longer suffering. The problem now was how to rejoin the regiment. The corporal remembered that HRH the Duke of Gloucester, who had visited Welbeck and knew the horse, was currently serving as liaison officer in France. He commandeered the stationmaster's phone and began the struggle to get his call through. Operators were at first incredulous and then rude, but Corporal Harrison was not to be denied. In due course a slightly ruffled royal duke was heard at the other end of the line, to be greeted by a Nottinghamshire voice: 'Sir, you remember that horse with a wart on his nose when you visited Welbeck?'

The Duke did remember, and out came

the corporal's story. There were immediate results. On the rear of the next train were coupled not only a straw-filled box for 'Wart Nose', but a carriage bearing three veterinary officers conjured up by His Royal Highness. Corporal Harrison and his horse reached Marseilles in ample time to rejoin their regiment.

One of the most disconcerting characteristics of the horse is his liability to sudden panic, often from seemingly trivial causes; when he does so, that primitive herd instinct, so often of value in a cavalry charge, results in mass hysteria among his fellows and stampede follows. At one time or another most mounted units experienced this terrifying and sometimes disastrous phenomenon—as did the Cheshire Yeomanry soon after they arrived in Palestine. One wet morning in February 1940 the horses of 'A' Squadron were being led out on exercise from their camp near Acre. Suddenly, for no apparent reason, the leading pair broke loose and galloped back down the column. Within

seconds the remainder followed suit and the sixty-odd animals thundered straight through an internee camp, scattering guards and prisoners, and bursting through two 7ft barbed-wire fences. They then headed for the coast, where the leaders hurtled over the cliffs, to be smashed on the rocks below. The rest of the day was spent in rounding up the survivors; many were so terribly lacerated by the barbed wire that they had to be destroyed immediately. The rest were evacuated to the veterinary hospital at Ramle, where many more were put down. The actual number lost is estimated at not less than thirty. Eyewitnesses reported that the charge of the 7ft double wire fence was led by a grey gelding which cleared the lot without touching a strand; an officer's charger transferred from the Greys, this horse was the only survivor

of the stampede without a scratch on his body. The cause of the panic was never established; some said the horses had sighted camels, others thought they had been startled by the men's capes flapping in the wind.

By the end of 1941 only two British cavalry regiments, the Cheshire Yeomanry and the Queen's Own Yorkshire Dragoons remained mounted. They had the unpleasant task of confronting former allies, the Vichy French, in Syria, but there was little action of consequence. After the French surrendered, these two regiments were mechanised; the Yorkshire Dragoons gave up their horses on 22 February 1942, and the Cheshires on 25 February. The Earl of Chester's Yeomanry can thus claim to be the last British cavalry regiment to have ridden horses on active service.

With the total mechanisation of the British cavalry in Palestine, some 6,000 horses became surplus. In addition, the British Army took over 1,200 horses, many of them in pitiable condition, from the Vichy French, who had abandoned them without water or food. Those still fit for duty were distributed among the horsed transport and pack units, some eventually serving in Italy, others in India and Burma. Not a single horse was sold in the Middle East; all those incapable of further service were humanely destroyed —thus the pledge extracted by Dorothy Brooke seven years previously was fully honoured.

In the Italian campaign of 1943–5 large numbers of animals were used by the British and American forces for mountain artillery and pack transport. The vast majority of these were mules; 'without pride of ancestry or hope of posterity' these animals have faithfully served the fighting soldier for almost as long as the horse. British mountain gunners used to swear by their 'long-eared darlin's' when

Cossack unit on exercise in a back area, 1944

it came to gruelling work on the old North-West Frontier of India, and even dedicated horsemen have admitted that the army mule could march a horse off his legs, with less in his belly.

After the occupation of Sicily in 1943, Major-General Lucian K. Truscott, an ex-cavalryman commanding the 3rd US Infantry Division, ordered the formation of a mounted reconnaissance troop. A varied assortment of horses was collected from the Italian cavalry stables at Palermo and from the local populace. Known as the 3rd Provisional Reconnaissance Troop, Mounted, it had five officers, 126 enlisted men and 143 horses, besides a supporting mountain artillery battery of four 75mm guns with 125 mules and a pack train of 349 mules. In the rugged mountainous country around Monte Cesimo—an impossible terrain for armour and difficult for infantry—this Troop proved the value of a mounted fighting force. In one sharp action it accounted for 105 Germans, with the loss of only thirteen men and thirty-one horses and mules. Later, General Patton observed: 'If we'd had a brigade or a division of horse cavalry in Sicily and Italy the bag of Germans would certainly have been bigger . . . As good as US armor was, the war could still have used some horses'.

For the record, it must be added that in 1943, during the Italian campaign, The King's Dragoon Guards formed an ad hoc troop for mounted patrol work, and this remained operational until the end of hostilities. It was purely a 'private' organisation, with no official authority; its strength never exceeded thirteen men and horses, and often dropped to four.

The greatest contribution made by horse and mule to the Allied war effort was undoubtedly in South-East Asia, where both were used on a huge scale for pack transport and, to a lesser degree, for reconnaissance work. In Burma the Chindits of General Wingate and the

Special Force units operating behind the Japanese lines depended almost entirely on horse (or pony) and mule for transport of supplies and ammunition. These operations saw the first large-scale airlift of animals in wartime: of the 500 horses and 3,000 mules employed, 2,216 were flown in to jungle air-strips, while many more were airlifted 'over the hump' to General Chiang Kai-Shek's forces in China.

The animals were carried in Dakota aircraft, four to a plane; contrary to expectations, both horses and mules proved to be trouble-free passengers, largely unaffected by altitude or engine roar. On one occasion two mules broke loose from their bamboo stalls and had to be destroyed. The unaccustomed mode of travel evidently had its effect on one pony mare; soon after touching down in the jungle she produced a foal, which was naturally named Free Drop.

The Burma theatre of operations presented the Royal Army Veterinary Corps officers with an unusual problem. The pack animals—particularly the mules—had a disconcerting trait of neighing and braying vociferously at awkward moments thus advertising a column's presence to the enemy. The veterinary authorities were asked to devise a 'devoicing' operation and in due course perfected a technique whereby the vocal cords were surgically removed under a general anaesthetic; between 1943 and 1945 more than 5,600 horses, ponies and mules were 'muted' before being flown out from India. This novel operation had no after-effects on the animals' performance. One veterinary officer reported that his own pony mare was on the march in the jungle within a week; in ten days she was carrying packs and, within fourteen days, wounded soldiers.

After the British retreat from Burma in

1942, four Indian infantry battalions were ordered to reorganise as 'light reconnaissance' units mounted on ponies; the last of these to retain their mounts was the 7th Battalion of the 10th Baluch Regiment. The task of initiating the 800 or so Punjabi, Dogra and Pathan sepoys into the mysteries of equitation on an assortment of shaggy hill-ponies (from Bhutan and Sikkim) was a daunting one—especially as many of the ponies proved to be in foal—but with the help of some British cavalrymen of the old school it was accomplished within the astonishingly short period of one month. Even if the unit's appearance on parade was, as one officer put it 'a motley one, calculated to startle even the most hardened Inspector-General of Cavalry', the battalion with its 728 ponies and 136 pack mules achieved some useful patrol work in the appallingly difficult country of the Chin Hills. Thus, while the Cheshire Yeomanry rightly claim to be the last regiment of British

A mule objects to his first air trip in a transport plane

cavalry to see active service on horseback, the last soldiers among the forces of the British Empire to do so as a formed regiment were those sepoys and officers of the 7/10th Baluch Regiment.

In 1944–5 the Allies were using 23,595 mules and 6,758 horses in South-East Asia Command. The Japanese too employed large numbers of animals—mostly horses and ponies—for transport and pack purposes. In their retreat through Burma in 1945, the 15th and 33rd Divisions lost more than 5,000, mainly from lack of forage; a Japanese veterinary officer admitted afterwards that of all the horses that set out on the advance on India only five returned to Thailand. He also said the best animals the Japanese obtained were the mules captured from the British forces.

After VJ Day, a number of RAVC officers were ordered to Thailand to

In some parts of the world the war horse still serves. This photograph, released in December 1974, shows a mounted unit of the Chinese People's Liberation Army on training in Sinkiang Province. The men carry swords as well as carbines

inspect and dispose of the surrendered Japanese animals; as Lieutenant-Colonel C. R. D. Grey reported in the *Journal of the United Service Institution of India* (1946), they were in a pitiable condition. At Bangkok 510 horses were found '. . . in an appalling state. A few were lying down quite unable to rise, while many had festering and flyblown sores . . . Over two-thirds were selected for immediate destruction'. The situation was worse 100 miles up country where the 37th Division had 2,699 horses; all but 545 were condemned and mercifully put down. As Colonel Grey observed, the Japanese concept of horsemastership was rudimentary, and characteristically inconsistent: no grooming seemed to be done, although boxes of unused brushes and curry combs abounded; manes and tails were long and matted; veterinary attention was limited to dabs of mercurochrome, despite ample stocks of veterinary equipment in beautifully fitted field chests; shoeing showed all the worst faults of 'dumping'—cutting

away heels and frog—and unnecessary rasping. Jap soldiers could often be seen squatting in front of their horses, with offers of green grass, but they appeared to ignore the animals' cut mouths, weeping eyes and festering sores. There was no bedding in stables—but there was an issue of sun-hats for the horses. 'When the animals were destroyed, many Japs stood at attention and saluted, and as the horse went down some wept.' Of the 5,227 horses inspected in Thailand, 3,691— just over 70 per cent—were destroyed.

The end of the war in Europe raised problems in the disposal of the enormous number of surrendered animals, but happily wholesale slaughter was not necessary. Lieutenant-Colonel J. C. Rix RAVC, who had the task of sorting out

58,000 horses handed over by the German army in Austria in May 1945, reported that the German cavalry units and their 'co-opted' Cossack brigade had looked after their animals extremely well. The few Croat and Hungarian units, however, had left theirs 'in a most pitiable state of emaciation'; evidently those Hungarians were unworthy of a nation which had once virtually lived on horseback. After being tested for disease, 44,476 horses were 'demobilised' and sent to help agricultural recovery in Italy, Germany, Austria and other countries. Only 3,000-odd were cast and destroyed; their flesh helped to feed the thousands of surrendered enemy troops and hordes of civilian refugees in the Carinthia district. General Patton had taken the Spanish Riding School of Vienna under his personal protection when the US forces reached Austria, and saved the matchless Lipizzaners from almost certain dispersal; he also arranged for the stud mares to be escorted back from Czechoslovakia where they had been sent by the German army.

The end of the war brought the final 'Slacken girths—File away to water' for most of the operational horsed units of the world's armed forces. But even in this computerised, press-button age there is still some use for the horse in war, although it is unlikely that the galloping squadrons will ever again thunder upon their foes with drawn swords and levelled lances. In jungle, scrub and mountainous regions —where the horseman has the advantage over mechanised troops for close reconnaissance purposes—the horse's cross-country mobility remains as valuable as ever.

The Chinese Peoples' Republic is reported to employ at least three divisions of horsed cavalry—or, more correctly, mounted infantry—for patrol work along her sensitive frontier with the Soviet Union; and there is little doubt that the Russians have similar forces on service in the same area. The Indian army maintains one regiment of operational horsed cavalry, which, together with a camel force, proves useful for patrol work in the Rajasthan desert area bordering Pakistan. The South African Defence Force has been raising mounted units to supplement mechanised patrols in the wild country of the Republic's northern frontiers. Until recently a regiment of Portuguese cavalry was operating in Angola and another in Mozambique. A *Daily Telegraph* correspondent, reporting from Mozambique, said that horses were less likely than vehicles to detonate the numerous land-mines sown by the insurgents—and added 'even if they do, the horse's stomach takes the main impact of the blast, leaving the rider safe . . .'

Horse-lovers everywhere will fervently hope that the days of large-scale employment of the horse on the battlefield are gone for ever. Sick, wounded, starved, he has patiently endured the horrors inflicted on him throughout the history of mankind's bitter quarrels, and has died in unrecorded millions. Let him now remain as our companion in sport and pleasure.

It is fitting to close this book with an extract from the moving tribute to the horse written by Ronald Duncan for London's Horse of the Year Show, 1954:

He serves without servility; he has fought without enmity. There is nothing so powerful, nothing less violent, there is nothing so quick, nothing more patient.
England's past has been borne on his back. All our history is his industry; we are his heirs, he our inheritance.

Bibliography

There is a vast body of literature on the horse, in war and peace. The following is a selective list of the major works that have proved of value in the writing of this book. Unless otherwise stated, place of publication is London.

Anderson, J. *Ancient Greek Horsemanship* (University of California, 1961)

Anglesey, The Marquess of. *A History of the British Cavalry* 2 vols (1973 and 1975)

Baker, Peter Shaw. *Animal War Heroes* (1933)

Baker, Lieut-Colonel Valentine. *The British Cavalry: with remarks on its Practical Organisation* (1858)

Billings, John D. *Hardtack and Coffee* (Boston, 1888)

Blunt, Lady Anne. *A Pilgrimage to Nejd* (1881)

—— *The Bedouin Tribes of the Euphrates* (1879)

Brooke, Mrs Geoffrey (Ed Glenda Spooner). *For Love of Horses: The Diaries of Mrs Geoffrey Brooke* (The Brooke Hospital for Animals, 1960)

Brown, D. A. *The Bold Cavaliers. Morgan's 2nd Kentucky Cavalry Raiders* (Philadelphia, 1959)

Burnaby, Colonel Fred. *Ride to Khiva* (1876)

Castillo, Bernal Diaz del. *Historia verdadera de la conquista de la Nueva España* (Mexico, 1904)

The Cavalry Journal (later *Armor*) (USA)

The Cavalry Journal (later *Journal of the Royal Armoured Corps*) (UK)

Child, Daphne. *Saga of the South African Horse* (Cape Town, 1967)

Childers, Erskine. *War and the Arme Blanche* (1910)

Clabby, Brigadier J. *The History of the Royal Army Veterinary Corps, 1919–1961* (1963)

Clode, Charles M. *The Military Forces of the Crown* 2 vols (1869)

Denhardt, R. M. *The Horse of the Americas* (University of Oklahoma, 1947)

Denison, Colonel G. T. *A History of Cavalry from the Earliest Times* (1913)

Douglas, Henry Kyd. *I Rode with Stonewall* (University of North Carolina, 1940)

Duffy, Christopher. *The Army of Frederick the Great* (Newton Abbot, 1974)

Felton, W. Sidney. *Masters of Equitation* (1962)

Fortescue, Hon J. W. *A History of the British Army* 13 vols (1899–1930)

Galtrey, Sidney. *The Horse and the War* (1918)

Goodall, Daphne Machin. *The Flight of the East Prussian Horses* (Newton Abbot, 1973)

Graham, R. B. Cunninghame. *The Horses of the Conquest* (1930)

Graham, Colonel W. A. *The Custer Myth. A Source Book of Custeriana* (New York, 1953)

Hamilton, Colonel H. B. *Historical Record of the 14th (King's) Hussars* (1901)

Harris, John. *The Gallant Six Hundred. A Tragedy of Obsessions* (1973)

Hayes, Captain H. M. *Points of the Horse* (1899)

Hope, Lieut-Colonel C. E. G. and Jackson, G. N. *The Encyclopaedia of the Horse* (1973)

Ingelfingen, Kraft Prinz zu Hohenlohe. *Conversations on Cavalry* (1896)

Jankovich, Miklós. *They Rode into Europe* (1971)

Journal of the Society for Army Historical Research

Kidd, James H. *Personal Recollections of a Cavalryman with Custer's Michigan Cavalry Brigade in the Civil War* (1908)

Lindsay, Major T. M. *History of the Sherwood Rangers in the 1939–45 War* (1952)

Lloyd George, David. *War Memoirs* (1933)

Luce, Captain Edward S. *Keogh, Comanche and Custer* (St Louis, 1939)

Lunt, James. *Charge to Glory!* (1961)

Marbot, Baron de (trans A. J. Butler). *Memoirs* (1892)

Markham, Gervase. *A Soldier's Accidence* (1617)

Maude, Lieut-Colonel F. N. *Cavalry: its Past and Future* (1903)

Mole, Edwin. *A King's Hussar* (1893)

Nolan, Captain L. E. *Cavalry: its History and Tactics* (1853)

Oman, Charles. *The Art of War in the Middle Ages* (1885)

Pennington, W. H. *Sea, Camp and Stage: incidents in the Life of a Survivor of the Balaclava Light Brigade* (1906)

Preston, Lieut-Colonel R. M. *The Desert Mounted Corps* (1921)

Simpson, G. G. *Horses. The Story of the Horse Family in the Modern World and through Sixty Million Years of History* (New York, 1951)

Smith, Maj-General Sir Frederick. *A History of the Royal Army Veterinary Corps 1796–1919* (1927)

Tomkinson, Lieut-Colonel W. *Diary of a Cavalry Officer in the Peninsular and Waterloo Campaigns* (1894)

Trench, Charles Chenevix. *A History of Horsemanship* (1970)

Tweedie, Maj-General W. *The Arabian Horse* (1894)

Tylden, Major G. *Horses and Saddlery* (1965)

Vaughan, Maj-General John. *Cavalry and Sporting Memories* (Bala, 1954)

Waley, Arthur (trans). *Secret History of the Mongols* (1963)

Wavell, Lieut-General Sir Archibald P. *The Palestine Campaigns* (1928)

Wentworth, Lady. *Thoroughbred Racing Stock* (1936)

—— *The Authentic Arabian Horse* (1945)

Xenophon (trans Morris H. Morgan). *The Art of Horsemanship* (1962)

Acknowledgements

The illustrations in this volume are reproduced by courtesy of the following: By gracious permission of Her Majesty the Queen, pp 31, 45, 79, 88; His Grace the Duke of Marlborough, p 66; His Grace the Marquess of Anglesey, p 74; Australian War Memorial, p 136; Bancroft Library, California, p 102; Mrs R. Blenman-Bull, pp 139, 140; British Museum, pp 15, 26, 34, 35; Fores Ltd, p 72; John R. Freeman & Co, pp 46, 47; Imperial War Museum, pp 122, 124, 128, 129, 130, 132, 135, 153; Mansell Collection, pp 9, 17, 18, 22, 55, 80, 81, 83, 85, 87, 100, 108, 141; Mary Evans Picture Library, p 101; Methuen (From Cecil G. Trew's *From 'Dawn' to 'Eclipse'*, 1939), p 7; Museo de America, Madrid, p 61; H. V. Musgrave Clark, p 118; National Army Museum, pp 67, 89, 94, 98, 115, 117, 121, 131; National Gallery, p 50; Novosti Press Agency, pp 150, 151, 152; Paul Popper, p 154; Radio Times Hulton Picture Library, p 112; Royal Artillery Depot, Woolwich, p 144; Royal Scots Dragoon Guards, p 127; Sabin Galleries, p 64; South African Tourist Corporation, p 133; Mrs L. Staveley, p 142; Tennessee State Museum, p 104; Franz Thiele, Hamburg, pp 147, 149; US Department of the Interior, p 113; US Signal Corps, p. 111; Victoria and Albert Museum, p 33; Wallace Collection, p 53; Zoological Society of London, p 8.

Further illustrations reproduced from drawings or paintings are as follows: p 73, drawing by Edouard Détaille; p 71, painting by O. Merté; p 126, painting by Lucy Kemp Welch; p 138, drawing by W. B. Wollen for *The Royal Artillery War Commemoration Book*, 1920.

Index

Index